Albert Maxfield, Robert Brady

Roster and Statistical Record of Company D

Of the Eleventh Regiment Maine InfantryVolunteers

Albert Maxfield, Robert Brady

Roster and Statistical Record of Company D
Of the Eleventh Regiment Maine InfantryVolunteers

ISBN/EAN: 9783337116477

Printed in Europe, USA, Canada, Australia, Japan

Cover: Foto ©ninafisch / pixelio.de

More available books at **www.hansebooks.com**

Roster and Statistical Record

—OF—

COMPANY D,

—OF THE—

Eleventh ❧ Regiment ❧ Maine ❧ Infantry ❧ Volunteers,

WITH A SKETCH OF ITS SERVICES

—IN THE—

WAR OF THE REBELLION.

PREPARED BY

ALBERT MAXFIELD AND ROBERT BRADY, JR.

"Far from over the distance,
The faltering echoes come :
Of the flying blast of bugle
And the rattling roll of drum."

1890.

In offering this Sketch, Roster and Statistical Record of the services of Company D in the War of the Rebellion, to its members, we wish to acknowledge the kind assistance given in its preparation by the men of D and of the Eleventh; also of that given by citizen friends in Maine, in tracing the fate of members of the Company who have wandered out of view in the twenty-five years that have passed since they were mustered out; and to acknowledge that of Captain Thomas Clark of the Office of the Adjutant-General of Maine, he having kindly furnished us with valuable and necessary information.

In reading the Sketch, members of D will kindly remember that it is written from one point of view only, and that many things they would like to see in it that are not there, may not have been sufficiently well remembered by the writer, if he ever knew them, to enable him to set them down in a trustworthy manner, and, too, that the limitations of space and the unity of the sketch made it necessary for him to leave out many things that he himself would have been glad to have incorporated in the story he had to tell.

The Roster and Statistical Record is as complete as it has seemed possible to make it. That there are blanks where there should be information is not at all the fault of the compiler, he having sought diligently but unsuccessfully for the information the blank spaces should furnish.

ALBERT MAXFIELD,
ROBERT BRADY, Jr.

COMPANY D,

—OF THE—

ELEVENTH REGIMENT MAINE INFANTRY VOLUNTEERS,

—IN THE—

WAR OF THE REBELLION.

This Company was formed in the early Fall of 1861. Its members were chiefly from the towns of the upper Penobscot, from Lee, Springfield, Topsfield, Enfield, Prentiss, and contiguous towns; a few from other parts of the State signing the Company rolls at Augusta.

According to its first descriptive list, much the greater number of the original members of D were farmers by occupation at the time of their enlistment, and most of them were young men of from eighteen to twenty-four years of age. And according to the same authority, its voluntary organization consisted of Leonard S. Harvey, Captain; John D. Stanwood, First Lieutenant; Gibson S. Budge, Second Lieutenant ; Robert Brady, First Sergeant ; with Abner F. Bassett, Jas. W. Noyes, Judson L. Young and Francis M. Johnson as Sergeants ; John McDonald, Richard W. Dawe, Ephraim Francis, Hughey G. Rideout, John Sherman, Benjamin Gould, Wm. H. Chamberlain and Freeman R. Dakin as Corporals ; Robert A. Strickland, Musician ; Henry W. Rider, Wagoner ; the rest of the Company, 77 in number, consenting to serve their country as private soldiers.

AUGUSTA AND WASHINGTON.

Thus organized, the Company rendezvoused at Augusta, where, October 19, '61, it was mustered into the service of the United States, as Company D, of the Eleventh Regiment Maine Infantry Volunteers.

The regiment started for Washington, November 13, '61, arriving there on the 16th, and the same day pitched its circular Ellis tents on Meridian Hill, back of Washington, naming its camp "Knox," after the hero of the Revolution that Maine claims as her own.

The only really notable event that took place in the several weeks the regiment occupied Camp Knox, was the Battle of the Sand Pits, by which name the quarrel between the men of the Eleventh and those of a United States Cavalry Regiment camped near Camp Knox, is known to the initiated. Whatever the cause of the quarrel, it culminated in an undisciplined rush to arms and a prompt occupation of the disputed sand pits by the more hot headed of the Eleventh. Fortunately no blood was shed before the officers of the two regiments got their men under control. No reputations were lost in this engagement, and but one was made, that of Private Longley, of D Company, who, with characteristic French-Canadian impetuosity slipped a cartridge into the muzzle of his Belgian rifle, bullet end first, effectually spiking the piece.

The Eleventh was here brigaded with the 104th and 52nd Pennsylvania, the 56th and 100th New York Infantry Regiments, Regan's Seventh New York Battery of three inch ordnance guns attached ; Colonel W. W. H. Davis, of the 104th Pennsylvania, in command of the Brigade, by reason of seniority of commission.

Soon after this formation, on New Year's Day, 1862, the brigade went into winter quarters in Carver Barracks, on Meridian Hill. Each regiment was domiciled in a dozen or fourteen one-story wooden houses, shell like structures of from fifty to sixty feet in length, twenty-five or thirty in width, and separated from each other by a street of perhaps twenty-five feet in width. The buildings of each regiment bordered one side of a great esplanade, the garrison flag floating from a tall staff in its center, each building laying a gable end to this square, which was common to all for drill and parade purposes.

Here the Winter was passed in perfecting the drill and discipline of the men, the officers gaining their technical military knowledge, book in hand, while imparting the contents to their stalwart pupils. In this way both officers and men practiced assiduously until they could load and fire in a truly military manner; march with mathematical accuracy and wheel geometrically. They also learned to obey orders without demur or question, under penalty of "Death or some worse punishment," as the men would have it the United States Army Regulations, read to them so frequently, provided for about all the offences in the military decalogue, this being their free rendering of the often closing phrase of a paragraph :—"Death, or such other punishment as the sentence of a court martial may inflict."

So far as recollection serves, the men of D were not given to law breaking. There is a remembrance though of Private Bridges standing on the head of a barrel at the head of the company street, a punishment for some now forgotten offense that did not seem to affect Private Bridges' sense of shame to any appreciable degree, he assuring all anxious inquirers that he was stationed in so commanding a position that he might announce the paymaster's anticipated approach from Washington, that all men of D might have timely warning to be on hand to receive their somewhat overdue dollars.

It was a very dull winter. About all the diversions from drill and parade that I recall are a few days on pass spent in wandering through the Capitol and other Government buildings—through the Smithsonian Institute—in visiting the already crowded hospitals—a marching part in the pompous military funeral given General Lander's body—and a dinner party given by D on Washington's Birthday, at which the field and staff of the regiment, the conspicuous guests, paid for their oyster stew and cider in speeches of impassioned eloquence, prophesying such a speedy downfall of the Wicked Rebellion that some of our men were almost inclined to pack their knapsacks before going to sleep, not to run any risk of missing the eastern train in the morning in case the W. R. should fall to pieces during the night.

This seems to be the place to have it recalled by Lieutenant Budge to the men of D who passed the Winter of 1861-62 in these barracks, that he commanded a detail that winter that, under the direction of the Provost Marshal General of Washington, seized and spilled into the gutters of that city some thirty thousand dollars worth of more or less ardent spirits. It would be interesting to have added to these figures a computation of the number of gallons of such fluids spilled by the men of D during its entire military history, spilled from canteens and other fluid receptacles, especially the number of gallons spilled by the re-enlisted men when on their famous furlough in the Winter of 1864.

Life in Washington passed as briefly indicated until March, when preparations were made for moving "On to Richmond." So eager were the men to make this movement, many of them fancying it would bring about an immediate ending of the war, that they chafed at the unavoidable delay that lack of transport service occasioned; Private Leighton, I believe it was, voicing the opinion of many that the delay was pusillanimous, and patriotically declaring for an immediate taking of Richmond and the hanging of Jeff. Davis, that all the farmers of the army might get home in time to attend to their Spring planting. And when there was one false start, the regiment in line, with baggage packed, and all ready for the word of command, then we were ordered back to quarters, there were curses loud and deep, even had been deacons using language that would have shocked the sisters, till the band jocularly struck up "Wait for the wagon and we'll all take a ride," when good nature was restored, proving that music indeed hath soothing charms.

THE PENINSULA CAMPAIGN.

The afternoon of the 28th of March, the brigade, now the third of General Casey's division of the Fourth Army Corps, General Keyes, commanding, was actually en route for Alexandria; Captain Maxfield's diary says :—"With boots blacked, hands in white gloves and brass shoulder scales on," a campaign guise difficult for the men of '64 to appreciate.

This was a hard march for green troops, unaccustomed to heavy marching order, with more too than the phrase implies, for besides gun, equipments, forty rounds of cartridges, the knapsacks were not only stuffed with the ordinary kits of soldiers, but were laden with the remains of civilian wardrobes and the accumulations of a winter's garrison duty. I think that no man of D ever reached a more welcome camp ground than the one outside of Alexandria that night. And by the time the newly issued shelter tents were buttoned together, were pitched, and the camp fires were lighted, there were many too weary to care for anything but to creep supperless into their tents, wrap their blankets around them and rest their aching bones. In the morning reveille awoke them to see a Spring snow storm, half rain and half snow beating down, followed by a day of discomfort and another night on a wet camp ground, and glad enough the next afternoon, that of March 30th, were all to get on board the transport Constitution, with all its discomforts of wet decks, on which the men must sleep closely crowded together; four regiments of our brigade, the Eleventh, the 56th and the 100th New York, and the 52d Pennsylvania regiments, with Regan's Battery, jamming the five decked Constitution to its utmost capacity.

Proceeding to Fortress Monroe, we were ordered to land at Newport News, to which place we were taken by a smaller steamer, the Constitution drawing too many feet of water to be able to reach the landing place. In steaming across the bay the masts of the sunken war ships could be seen standing above the surface of the water telling of the great Naval combat that so lately took place in this placid water. Soon a puff of smoke rolled out from a rebel battery off Sewall's Point, announcing the coming of the first hostile shot. It fell so far short of our steamer that the tell-tale spray of water its plunge threw into the air was received by us with a yell of derision.

Landing at Newport News the 2d of April, the brigade went into camp, where we remained for a few days owing to lack of wagon transportation. It was here that the men first went on picket. And Captain Maxfield's diary records that there was a rush among them to go on picket duty, probably as great a one as there was in later years to escape such service.

The 6th of April, we proceeded to Young's Mills, where we occupied the log barracks rebel troops had occupied the previous winter. Here the regiment was paid off, and where they had learned it is a mystery, but it did seem as if not only the men of D but those of every company of the regiment were adepts in the mysteries of the national game ; for wherever you went through the thick woods surrounding the barracks you would come across groups of men squatting around the tops of hard bread boxes laid on the ground, and hear such mystic phrases as :—"Ante up or leave the board." "It's your deal." "I raise you five cents." "I see you and go you five better." Some of the men wrecked their available fortunes in a few hours at the game, then would borrow a quarter from some friend and regain all they had lost, only to lose it again before night. Such is the see-saw of fortune.

The 17th of April, we rejoined the brigade in position before Lee's Mill, on the creek known as the Warwick River. We took a modest part in the siege of Yorktown. I chiefly remember a reconnoissance in which Company D followed a skirmish line as its reserve.

By company front, trying to keep a perfect alignment, keeping step as if on parade, D crashed through woods and bushes, quite undaunted until a shell came screeching towards them ; and as it fell some twenty feet before them, burst in a cloud of smoke and the pieces went flying into the air, our heroes waited with open mouths for half a minute perhaps, certainly quite long enough for all danger to have passed, then at one and the same time each and all, as if by a common impulse, threw themselves flat upon the ground, and digging their noses into the soil, lay there for another full half minute before arising to march on their dignified way.

Think of that you men of Morris Island, to whom flying shot and shells became a matter of course, of no more consequence than beans from a bean shooter. But that was your first shell, and 'twas long before you had heard the warning cries of "Jim Island" and "Sullivan," long before those names had become so familiar to you as to have hardened your nerves to comparative indifference.

It was in this reconnoisance that the first man of the regiment was killed, Private Mace, of Company A. As the first man of the regiment killed, his body had a fascination for all of us as it lay in camp, and few of us but were awe struck as we looked upon the waxen face of our comrade, now drained of blood, but yesterday blooming with health and spirits, struck dead in a second as if by a thunderbolt. The only other matter for record here is our being called out early one morning to stand to arms and listen to the attack a portion of the Vermont brigade made on the dam across the Warwick, known as Dam No. 1. Though the charging and the answering yells, the crash of musketry and the booming of cannon came to us, out of danger, but as the crash and uproar of a distant thunder shower, yet it was so suggestive of what was going on in the semi-darkness beyond the intervening woods, that it gave some of us a dread foreboding that the time was really near at hand when we must be active participants in just such bits of the bloody game of war.

We were not in the trenches before Yorktown at any time except as individuals. Then to creeping to the outer works and watching the slow operations of the siege, we much preferred to sit in the interior works and listen to the blood-curdling tales of the so-called California sharpshooters, the butts of whose rifles were notched to their utmost capacity, each notch representing a dead rebel, according to its owner's statement, but as it was estimated that the combined notches on the butts of their rifles outnumbered the entire rebel force under Magruder, it is more probable that they bore quite as much testimony to the mendacious abilities of the story tellers as to their sharp shooting ones.

One fine May morning, that of the 4th, it was known that Magruder had evacuated Yorktown the night before, and under the command of our new brigade commander, Brigadier General Henry M. Naglee, we were in quick pursuit. We crossed the rebel lines at Lee's Mills, which fortified position we gallantly carried without loss in the absence of the flying enemy.

As the different commands of our army moved forward, they converged on the road leading from Yorktown to Williamsburg with the result that this road was soon packed with horse, foot and artillery, all pushing eagerly forward, and without overmuch regards for right of way.

Company D, holding the right of the regiment, was a pleased auditor to a little conversation between Colonel Caldwell and the irate commander of a regiment the Eleventh had unceremoniously displaced. The displaced commander was evidently, by manner and seat in the saddle, a regular officer, which then meant among other things, an officer with large ideas of his own importance as a trained military man, and small ones of all volunteer officers.

"Sir," roared he, riding up to Colonel Caldwell, "How dare you march across the head of my command?"

The Colonel looked at him in his large placid way, without answering him, much as a mastiff looks at a snarling terrier.

"Do you know who I am, sir?" yelled the angry commander, now doubly enraged at the elaborate indifference, and the apparently studied silence of our Colonel. "I am Major so-and-so of such and such a regiment."

"And I," answered Colonel Caldwell, smiling blandly, touching his cap with military courtesy as he spoke, "And I am Colonel John C. Caldwell, commanding the Eleventh Maine Regiment of Infantry Volunteers, and am quite at your service, sir."

Speechless with rage, and fairly gasping at the haw-haw of approval we country bumpkins gave the Colonel's answer, Major so-and-so backed his horse a little, turned him, and galloped away in as furious a state of mind as any gallant Major ever galloped in.

This bright May day was spent by the infantry in marching and halting while the cavalry pressed forward on the heels of the flying enemy. Towards night the regiments went into bivouac. Then the men scattered for foraging purposes. The inhabitants had mainly fled to Richmond, perhaps naturally, they consisting of women, children and male antiquities generally, McClellan's report stating that every able bodied male of the Peninsula was in the ranks of the rebel army.

They went hastily, evidently. I remember one house from which the occupants had fled just as they were about to seat themselves to a meal apparently, for the table was spread with dishes and untouched victuals. Loading themselves with food and furniture from these deserted houses, the boys returned to camp.

My particular group of D slept that night on a feather bed, spread on the ground, with sheets, quilts, pillows—all the accompaniments. But, alas, it began to rain heavily in the night, so that before morning our downy nest of the evening before was about as comfortable a sleeping place as a bed-tick filled with mush and milk would be—a soaked, oozing, nasty mess.

In the morning we pushed forward in a heavy rain over roads cut up by artillery wheels and punched full of holes by the hoofs of innumerable horses. We could soon hear the battle of Williamsburg progressing in front as we, wet to the skin, plodded on our miserable way. Towards night, General McClellan ordered General Naglee to push forward and reinforce General Hancock, who was reported as heavily pressed. We moved forward rapidly and zealously, but before we could reach Hancock, that brilliant commander had, by feigning a retreat, led the opposing enemy from their intrenchments into the open field, where with a few heavy volleys he stopped them, then charging with the bayonet, routed and dispersed their column, capturing some five hundred of it.

We arrived only in time to witness the overthrow of the enemy, and to give the victors generous cheers of congratulations. Taking position in line, we stood to our arms through a cold, wet night, entirely without fire, and almost without food, our nearly empty haversacks furnishing us with a very scanty supper. It was a night to remember.

But in the morning, the dreaded morning, when all that long line of earth-works, beyond which lay the old city of Williamsburg, must be carried ; in the morning our chilled blood was not only warmed by a brilliant sun, but by the knowledge that the Confederates had evacuated these intrenchments too, and were still falling back towards Richmond.

The supply trains had been left behind in leaving the lines before Yorktown, and when enterprising wagon-masters did get their trains towards the front, they were compelled to give way to hurrying troops and artillery. It now became necessary to await the coming of these but lately despised supply trains, for soldiers,

9

to march and fight, must be fed, and you might as well try to get fight out of empty cartridge boxes as out of empty haversacks.

A few days then, we of necessity spent before Williamsburg, to rest the exhausted troops and to replenish empty cartridge boxes and haversacks. These few days were mainly passed by our men in taking a first sight of the horrors of war. Not only our own wounded were there, but the enemy's as well, left behind in the care of their surgeons, in the hurried flight of the rear guard that had made the stand for delay at Williamsburg. Cut, hacked, shot, dead and dying, a sorry sight there was in the barracks Confederate troops had occupied during the winter, now used for hospital purposes. And out on the field was a worse one. Dead bodies lay where they fell, and as they fell. Some in the act of loading, some as if firing, these that had been shot dead in their tracks; others lay on their backs or curled into tortuous shapes, staring stonily, as if for a last look at the world that had faded from their darkening eyes as the life blood poured from their mortal wounds. However hardened we became afterwards, the most indifferent of us by nature was then visibly affected by the gruesome sights we saw on the bloody field of Williamsburg.

The 9th of May we were on the march again, but moved slowly, the roads being few and narrow, and the weather rainy. On the 13th, Colonel Caldwell having been promoted a Brigadier-General, took leave of us and Colonel Plaisted assumed command. It was two o'clock in the morning of the 14th of May before we reached New Kent Court House, and about the 19th before we reached the Chickahominy and took possession of the ruins of Bottoms and the Railroad Bridges.

A reconnoissance D and a piece of artillery made showed that the last named bridge had been burned. We had a merry exchange of grape with the enemy's artillery across the river, here about forty feet wide, fringed with a dense growth of forest trees, and bordered by low marshy bottom lands, varying from half a mile to a mile in width, as McClellan describes it. The following day, the 20th, Naglee's Brigade crossed Bottoms Bridge and D with another company of infantry and a squadron of cavalry followed General Naglee for some miles along a road leading through White Oak Swamp to the James River. We touched the enemy's cavalry but once and quickly formed at a bridge to receive his anticipated charge. It not coming, General Naglee crossed the bridge with his cavalry and charged the enemy, the General at the head of his little force scattering the enemy in every direction but ours. We then marched on again for some miles, when the infantry went into position at a big farm house on a commanding hill and General Naglee and the cavalry rode away towards the James River. It was said that they watered their horses in that river before returning to us, which they did in about an hour. We then made a rapid retrograde movement for Bottoms Bridge, marching back by another road than that we had taken in advancing, by this sharp maneouvre escaping the attention of a body of gray coated gentlemen who had assembled at a point on our line of advance to give us a taste of Southern hospitality on our return march. This rapid and brilliant reconnoissance, right through the enemy's country, gave General McClellan important information regarding roads and their connections that he found very useful to him when unexpected circumstances forced us to retreat in that direction.

On the 24th of May, General Naglee's brigade dislodged the enemy from the vicinity of Seven Pines and secured a strong position for our advance. McClellan says also that on the 25th, under cover of a movement by General Naglee, the whole Fourth Corps took up and began to fortify a position at Seven Pines. On the 28th his record also shows Casey's division was moved forward to Fair Oaks, three-quarters of a mile in advance of Seven Pines, leaving General Couch at the works at Seven Pines. General Casey immediately began a new line of rifle pits and a small redoubt for six field guns to cover our new position. Here we were engaged in constant skirmishing and picket service until May 31, when the battle of Fair Oaks was fought. When about noon of the 31st of May the Rebel Commanders of D. H. Hill, Huger, Longstreet and G. W. Smith swept down on Casey's division, D and other companies of the regiment were on the picket line, D on the extreme right. The few members of D left in camp joined regiments moving to the front as they came forward, and with the rest of Naglee's Brigade, to use the language of General McClellan's official report concerning our brigade, "struggled gallantly to maintain the redoubt and rifle pits against the overwhelming masses of the enemy." As individuals those of D so engaged did their duty, both here and in the later stands made at General Couch's rifle pits. One of them, Private Gray, reported missing, was undoubtedly killed while voluntarily attached to some stranger organization, receiving burial with their dead of his adopted regiment. But the story of D as a company we will tell from information furnished us by its First Sergeant, Brady, who commanded and directed its movements when it made its stand on the picket line against an advancing line of battle. The portion of the Regiment not on picket was taken into the battle by then Major Campbell, and shares with the 104th Pennsylvania the warm encomiums of official writers on the heroic bravery shown by these two regiments that day.

The night before the battle of Fair Oaks was one of a terrible storm, that we all know. D went on picket that evening, occupying the extreme right of the line, an entirely unsupported position. The men passed a miserable night, watching in darkness and storm, sheltering themselves as they best could and still remain alert, for all the signs pointed to an early attack on us; the pressure of the enemies skirmish lines, the plain movements of their troops, and the fact that they must either dislodge us or lose Richmond. Towards morning the storm ceased, and the day broke with the promise of clearness. Shortly afterwards Sergeant Brady came out of camp with Private Annis, then a detailed cook, Annis bearing a camp kettle in which he proceeded to prepare coffee, when the men partook of a rough breakfast. Soon Lieutenant Washington, of General Johnston's staff, rode unexpectedly into the line of D, having mistaken a road in carrying orders to some rebel command. Quickly halted, he ruefully yielded himself a prisoner, and under Captain Harvey's pilotage made an unwilling way to General Casey's headquarters. Captain Harvey failing to return, the command of the company devolved upon Second Lieutenant Johnson, as First Lieutenant Stanwood was away sick. The capture of Lieutenant Washington made the pickets doubly alert. Besides, General Naglee himself rode out to their line to make observations, and warned them that they were liable to be attacked at any moment. Soon great activity was displayed by the rebel pickets in the immediate front, and sharp picket fighting took place during the forenoon. A little after noon the roar of the attack on the left was heard. It was uncertain what the pickets should do. Lieutenant Johnson and Corporal Keene moved out on the right to learn, if they could, what force, if any, guarded the flank. They found it entirely unguarded, and moved along until they fell in with Sumner's advance, when they were occupied in giving information concerning the movements of the enemy, and the bearing of the roads to General Sumner's aids.

Sergeant Brady had been left in command of the company by Lieutenant Johnson, and shortly a rebel line of battle appeared moving towards the line held by D. Under Sergeant Brady's orders, some of the men began to barricade the road they centered on by falling trees across it, the others keeping up a rapid fire on the enemy to give the idea by their boldness that they covered a line of battle, while really between them and Fair Oaks there was then no force whatever. This ruse succeeded to an unexpected degree, the rebel line of battle halting, throwing out a strong skirmish line, and making an elaborately cautious advance. Of course their skirmishers easily flanked our forlorn pickets, and curling them back in spite of their stubborn resistance, finally scattered them through the woods.

Before the rebel onset, Sergeant Brady, realizing by the sound of the battle that he was cut off from his camp, had carefully cautioned the men to make their line of inevitable retreat toward the right and rear, and fortunately for most of them they followed these orders, reaching our lines in safety. Those that were captured were Sergeant Bassett, Corporal Dakin, Musician Strickland, Privates William and Moses Sherman, House, and lastly Sergeant Brady himself, who, the captor of two rebel soldiers, was triumphantly following his prisoners into our lines as he supposed, when, reaching the railroad, a line of rebel infantry confronted him, and he found it necessary to exchange place with his own prisoners, who, you may be sure, took a great pleasure in escorting him to Richmond. These, with Private Gray killed, and Private Blaine wounded, cover the loss of D at the battle of Fair Oaks.

It will be seen by this, that when night fell on the first day of the battle of Fair Oaks, Company D was somewhat scattered. Some of its members had joined the colors, but many were still wandering in search of them, while a stout detachment was already housed in Libby Prison. But before the next day noontime, the company was fully organized again under the command of Lieutenant Johnson, Captain Harvey relinquishing the command, pending the acceptance of his resignation, which circumstances forced him to send in.

The regiment took no part in the second day's fighting, constituting part of the reserve. That night they lay in the edge of a piece of woods. During it certain mules belonging to the Q. M. Department of our army were stampeded, galloping in a body along our line of battle, the rattling of the chains of their harnesses which had not been removed when they where unhitched from the wagons, so resembling the clanking of the scabbards of galloping cavalrymen, that many of the Eleventh, more than will confess it, were sure that the rebel Stuart and his cavalry were upon us. For a few minutes the utmost consternation and confusion prevailed, but the truth was quickly known and quiet restored. Of course no one was really scared, still it is said that some of the Eleventh, and they not all of the rank and file either, displayed an unexpected aptitude for tree climbing during the misconception.

After the battle we had occasion to look over the battle-field, for of course we did not know that our missing were captured, they might be killed or wounded.

It told the same ghastly story of war as that of Williamsburgh. Our hastily abandoned camp had been rummaged by the Confederates and the shelter tents and old blankets taken from it to spread on the wet ground as they lay in line of battle. The long line of wet trampled tents and blankets told the exact position the enemy occupied the night of the first day of the battle. The kettles still hung over the charred embers of the extinguished cook fires, the headquarters' tents still stood in their places, the horns of the band still hanging on the limbs of the apple trees they were hanging on when the band took its hasty departure for Augusta. It tooted for us no more. In a day or two our division was placed under command of General Peck and ordered to guard the Railroad Bridge and Bottoms Bridge ; Couch's division guarding the fords across the White Oak Swamp. For some days our position was at the bridges, we camping at the end of the Railroad Bridge, just where the Confederate artillery had stood when D and its Federal piece of artillery first opened fire on each other from opposite ends of the bridge. Then came the swift and almost unheralded march of Jackson from the Valley to the south side of the Chickahominy and the Seven Days' Battles. The story of the Battle of Gaines' Mills was brought to us by the seemingly interminable army of the disheartened troops that for hours filed across the Railroad Bridge, without officers or orders, clamoring that all was lost, and that Jackson was moving swiftly towards us, crushing all opposition.

With a well-manned battery, strongly supported, placed on the hill behind us, the Eleventh went down into the swamps of the Chickahominy, remaining there in a long skirmish line for two or three days, expecting every hour to hear the skirmishers of the enemy crashing through the woods of the opposite shore of the Chickahominy, now easily fordable by light troops. But before the momentarily uncertain enemy moved forward McClellan's rapidly laid plans had been fully acted on, our right wing was across the Chickahominy by its various bridges, the bridges were destroyed, and the retreat to the James River was in full operation. As we moved away from the Railroad Bridge, the center spans of which had been destroyed by axemen of the Eleventh the day before, the famous train of cars that our men had loaded with shells and combustibles at Savage Station came tearing down the track, and reaching the bridge took its mighty header.

General "Dick" Taylor, of the Confederates, who was in command of the troops at the other end of the bridge, says of it, while the battle of Savage Station was raging on the afternoon of June 29th, Magruder attacking Sumner, to be beaten off, the din of the distant combat was silenced to his ears by a train approaching from Savage Station, gathering speed as it rushed along, quickly emerging from the forest to show two engines drawing a long string of cars. Reaching the bridge, the engines exploded with a terrible noise, followed in succession by the explosion of the carriages laden with ammunition. Shells burst in all directions, he says, the river was lashed into foam, trees were torn for acres around, and several of his men were wounded.

To this harsh music we moved swiftly away till we had crossed White Oak Swamp Bridge in gathering darkness and reached the high ground beyond it. Here we bivouacked in line of battle, all but the guards sleeping on their arms, while the rear guard came filing across the bridge. In the morning exhausted troops could be seen lying fast asleep everywhere—in the fields, the woods, even in the dusty road itself. But all of our troops were across the swamp, and as fast as the packed condition of the roads to the James would permit, all but those of us to form the rear guard of the day, the divisions of Smith and Richardson and Naglee's Brigade, under command of Franklin, to lay here and hold Jackson himself at bay, were moving slowly towards the next selected position to make a stand—Malvern Hill. That Jackson was on the other side of the bridge we knew, the rattle of the skirmishers' rifles told us that. But just about noon he announced his presence by suddenly opening on us with thirty pieces of artillery.

One moment there was nothing above us but a cloudless summer sky, the next the air was full of shrieking shells, bursting in puffs of white smoke, and showering down a storm of broken iron. It was so startling in its suddenness that it is not strange, as the Second Corps chronicler says, that there was "a scene of dire confusion." And to add to it, the men in charge of a ponton train drawn up by the roadside, waiting for an opportunity to lumber away along it, unhitched their horses, mounted them and fled for the James River.

The confusion lasted but for a minute, and in it the Eleventh had no share. We were lying in the edge of the woods that bordered the great cleared field in which the troops and trains were massed, and perhaps had an advantage in all being wide awake. At any rate we were not a bit demoralized. Scarcely a man started to his feet, all waiting for the word of command. It came quickly, and from the mouth of General Naglee himself, who riding up to us and seeing our immovability while the troops around us were in evident confusion, could not restrain his delight at our coolness, but cried out "Fall in, my Yankee squad," for the Eleventh was few in numbers now. We fell in, and as he proudly led us across the big field to a new position, we stiffened our necks and neither dodged or bowed to the storm of iron beating down upon us. We had made a hit, and we knew it.

Taking up a position behind the rails of a torn-down fence, the Eleventh lay listening to Jackson's cannon and watching Hazzard's battery as it swept the White Oak Swamp Bridge with a storm of grape and cannister that kept even Jackson at bay. The cannoneers fell one by one—were thinned out until the officers not yet killed or wounded dismounted and took their places at the guns.

It was whispered that their ammunition was giving out—was most gone—a few rounds more and the last shell would be fired, and then Jackson and his 35,000 men would pour across the bridge and up the heights to learn what sort of stuff we were made of.

But this was not to be. Just as we were gathering ourselves together for the apparently fast coming struggle, there came a yell from the rear, a sound of desperately galloping horses, and with slashing whips Pettits' battery came tearing on at the top of their horses' speed, General Naglee leading them into position. Ours, as did all the regiments massed in the big field, rose and cheered Naglee and the artillerymen as they swept by. Inside of a minute from their first appearance, they were in position, unlimbered, and were sweeping the bridge with grape and cannister.

Away on the left, at Glendale, there was fighting, and hard fighting too. Our men were so hard pressed that Franklin felt obliged to return two brigades to Sedgwick that he had borrowed from him. And our old commander, Colonel Caldwell, who had been with us during the day (now a Brigadier-General and commanding a brigade in Richardson's division), marched away with his brigade too, and rendered effective service in beating the masses of the enemy off.

They attacked at several points in their efforts to break through the lines of our men covering the roads by which our supply, ammunition and artillery trains were retreating to Malvern Hill. Slocum, on the Charles City road, was attacked at half-past one o'clock, but held his position by a sweeping artillery fire. Then, McCall, at Glendale, a point half way to Malvern Hill, was heavily attacked. McCall and many of his men and guns were captured, but the strength of the rebel blow was exhausted in the necessary effort, so that Sumner, whose line had been in the rear of McCall's, letting the broken troops through, opened heavily with artillery and musketry, repulsing all the enemy's efforts to break his line. Later in the day an attempt was made on Porter, stationed at Malvern Hill. He, too, by the aid of the gunboats, maintained his position. As night fell, we prepared to retreat. The abandoned pontoon train was set on fire, and by its flaring light we moved back, marching on and on until morning found us in position with our own division at Malvern Hill.

The line of battle stretched around Malvern Hill, which is a point on the James River of perhaps sixty feet in height with a broad cleared top. Our line of defence made a huge semicircle, the flanks on the river and under protection of the gunboats. Our own position was on the right flank, close to the river. But a third of the troops of our army were actually engaged in the battle of July 1st, 1862. It was an artillery battle; the hill was crowned with sixty pieces of artillery, planted to sweep all possible openings by which troops could advance. Magruder and D. H. Hill made determined efforts to withstand their fire but, when supplemented with a rolling infantry fire, no troops could stand it. Night fell with our position undisturbed at any point.

As for me, I slept through most of the uproar; slept the sleep of the thoroughly tired-out. And I understand that all that could of the army did so too, refreshing tired Nature against the hour of need; many of the troops actually engaged waking to do their brief part in repelling an assault, and that done, to lie down in their line of battle to fall asleep again.

When darkness set in the retreat was continued. Troops, batteries and trains moved towards Harrison's Landing all night. Morning broke, the heavens opened, and torrents of rain descended. Our division lay in a covering position to oppose any advance the enemy might make, but he had given up the chase. With our troops already on the James, under cover of our gunboats, he knew it was madness to pursue further. So, the sodden, tired men, the trains of wounded, batteries and wagons floundered unmolested through the mud into Harrison's Landing, and not till all were past us, the last straggling man and wagon, did we of the rear guard move into that haven of rest and safety for the beaten, battered, exhausted Army of the Potomac.

HARRISON'S LANDING.

At Harrison's Landing our regiment was encamped on the left of the line, close to the river. There was but one alarm here, that of the morning of August 1, when the enemy ran some light guns to the opposite bank of the James and opened fire on the landing. For about thirty minutes there was a lively exchange of shot and shell between their battery and our gunboats, when the enemy fell back, and troubled us no more.

Here we remained until the middle of August, our life a monotony of picket duty in an open field, baking, sweltering under a hot sun, with only such shelter as kennels made of sticks and wheat straw afforded. In camp, a well shaded one fortunately, we lazily slept the time away, drilling occasionally, but not often, though when General Emory took command of our brigade here, General Naglee going north on leave, he established a series of brigade drills, the chief amusement in which, to the rank and file, was to see the commanders of the different regiments gallop up to the General after each awkward movement to receive the maledictory criticisms of that outraged old cavalry warrior on their evident ignorance of what to him was as familiar as winking. They passed his enconiums along to their line officers on returning to their regiments you may be sure, and the line officers took it out of their "non coms," who cursed the men for their stupidity, who damned the man who invented tactics and themselves for having been such fools as to enlist for soldiers with which officers could play shuttlecock and battledore.

Finally, the preparations for the evacuation of the Landing being completed, we of Keyes' Corps moved away from it the 16th of August. The 17th we crossed the Chickahominy near the mouth of the James, crossing on a ponton bridge of two thousand feet in length, reached Williamsburg the 18th, went into camp about where we did when there in May, marching to Yorktown the 20th.

YORKTOWN.

All of the army but two divisions of our corps now took transports to go to the relief of Pope and Burnside, and to fight the battle of Antietam. Two divisions of our corps were left on the Peninsula; Couch's going with the main army. Our brigade took position at Yorktown, and proceeded to strengthen the defences of that place to enable it to resist any attack from the direction of

Richmond. The work was soon completed, but we were not troubled by the enemy. Once a raid of Confederate cavalrymen on Williamsburg created a flurry of anticipation, but nothing came of it except an opportunity for General Emory to see the regiments promptly take their previously assigned positions. The General soon after this left us, General Naglee having returned, and it was known that though General Emory had taken command reluctantly, preferring his old command naturally, yet that he left us with characteristic and vigorous asseverations of regret at having to do so. Shortly before his leaving, the so-called "'62 men " joined us. Their recruits were rather looked down on at first by the "veterans" of one campaign, and for a time were kept in open-mouthed admiration by a few true, and many apochryphal, stories of the valor and endurance the story-tellers declared they themselves had so lately displayed. The men of '62 that D received were all good men and true, and added no little to the good fellowship of the company as well as to its strength. Many of them coming from seaboard towns, some of them seafaring men, they brought a new and rather desirable element, a jovial, adventurous one, into the ranks, until now almost entirely made up of plodding farmers.

Two expeditions were fitted out from Yorktown, in both of which D took a part, one to Matthews County and the other to Gloucester Court House. As Captain Maxfield, then a private of Company C, was an active participant in both these movements, and the compiler of these sketches was in neither, Captain Maxfield will tell of what befell the troops of these expeditions.

MATTHEWS COUNTY.

Nov. 22, '62. Nine companies of the regiment left camp between 8 and 9 p. m., and embarking on the gunboats Mahaska and Putnam and the tug-boat May Queen, proceeded down the York River and up the Chesapeake Bay. They entered the Mob Jack Bay about 8.30 a. m. on the 23d, and proceeded up the East River, where they landed in Matthews County, Va., at 11.30 a. m. The force was divided and sent to different plantations, where they destroyed large quantities of salt and salt works, or salt kettles. The male portion of the community were taken and held as prisoners while we remained. The writer was in the detachment commanded by Captain Libby of Company A, and went to the plantation of Sands Smith. We shall never forget the warlike picture of little Pete Neddo of Company A breaking the big kettles with a sledge hammer, or the poor old negro woman, whose son had run away a few months previous and had accompanied us as one of the guides of the expedition, at sight of the boy. She threw herself on her knees and with hands upraised, exclaimed " Is this Jesus Christ ! Is it God Almighty !" Nor could we refrain from expressing the wish that this "cruel war" was over when we made prisoners of the old gentleman and the young men who had come to his house to spend the pleasant Sunday afternoon in the society of his lovely daughters. We returned to the gunboats soon after dark.

At 9 a. m. on the 24th, as we were about getting under way for our return, a farmer came in with a flag of truce, who said a supply train was passing at a short distance and could be easily captured. The force on the Putnam, consisting of Companies A, C and D, was landed, and under command of Captain S. H. Merrill of Company I, ordered to reconnoitre for one hour. We advanced about three miles, which brought us in sight of Matthews Court House, where there appeared to be a small force. After commencing our retreat we found we were pursued by a body of cavalry. Lieutenant F. M. Johnson and Corporal J. F. Keene of Company D, who allowed themselves to be separated from the command, were taken prisoners. We immediately returned to Yorktown, where we arrived about sundown.

No field officer of the Eleventh accompanied this expedition, it being under the command of Major Cunningham of the Fifty-second Pennsylvania Volunteers.

GLOUCESTER COURT HOUSE.

Dec. 11, '62. The regiment left camp before sunrise, crossed the York River to Gloucester Point, and in company with the Fifty-second Pennsylvania, Fifty-sixth and One Hundredth New York, and Battery H, First New York Artillery, took up the line of march for Gloucester Court House, where we arrived at 4 p. m. We remained in the vicinity of the Court House, sending out foraging parties in different directions, who captured herds of cattle, sheep, mules and some fine horses. The cavalry, which led the advance from Gloucester Point, advanced to within a few miles of the Rappahannock. The expedition was commanded by General Henry M. Naglee, and was intended as a diversion in rear of the rebel army during the battle of Fredericksburg.

We commenced our retreat just after sunset on the 14th, and arrived in camp at 3.30 a. m. on the 15th, without the loss of a man, bringing our captured herds and the prisoners captured by the cavalry.

One of the incidents of this expedition occurred when a member of the Eleventh attempted to pay for certain articles of food at a house near the Court House. The occupant absolutely refused to accept greenbacks, but one of his comrades perceiving the dilemma, produced a bill on the Bank of Lyons Kathairon, a patent medicine advertisement, which the lady readily received, supposing it to be genuine Confederate money.

THE DEPARTMENT OF THE SOUTH.

In December we began to hear rumors that our brigade was to take part in an expedition to the further South, and soon active preparations for a movement were going on around us. The sick were sent North, ammunition and other supplies were plentifully provided, transports began to swing at anchor in the bay, and the 26th of the month we of the Eleventh found ourselves sailing away on the old steamer Cahawba in company with the 98th New York, General Naglee and staff, and the brigade band, bound for Morehead City, where we arrived the first day of January, 1863.

We had a stormy passage, especially off Cape Hatteras. Here we saw the original Monitor in tow of the transport steamer Rhode-Island, passing closely enough to them towards night to see the heavy seas washing over the Monitor's low decks, to the evident discomfort of the bare-legged seamen. Before morning the Monitor had gone down, but her crew was saved by the Rhode-Island.

We landed at Morehead City and marched to Carolina City, a few miles away, where we went into camp. The term city as applied to these and other Southern places is usually mighty misleading. For example, Carolina City consists even now of little more than a railroad depot, and Morehead City is but a little larger.

Our brigade remained comfortably encamped at Carolina City for a few weeks, our idea being that we were intended to form part of a force to descend upon Wilmington.

And, when the Eleventh went on board the Cahawba again, this time in company with the 104th Pennsylvania instead of the 98th New York, and put to sea in company with a fleet of transports carrying our new division, we thought that Wilmington was our objective point. General Naglee, now the commander of the division our expedition consisted of, was on board the Cahawba with his staff, as was Colonel Davis, now again in command of our brigade, and his staff. We soon learned that we were bound for Port Royal, S. C., and that to capture Charleston was the object of our expedition.

But though we went on board the Cahawba the 20th day of January, it was not till the afternoon of the 29th that we put to sea. We arrived at Port Royal January 31st, and entering the harbor, found ourselves one of a large and growing fleet of transports and gunboats. The 3d of February we sailed up Port Royal Sound to Beaufort, where we landed that the Cahawba might be cleaned, then reembarked on it the next day and returned to Port Royal. We were not landed again for some days, and the warm Southern sun operating on men as crowded together as we were, without opportunity for exercise and proper cleanliness, was not conducive to good health. Sickness cropped out, ship fever prevailed to an alarming extent, and a number of the Eleventh died before the troops were landed at St. Helena Island, which they were on the 10th of February. Landing, our regiments went into camp, and winter as it was, we found it necessary to cover our tents with an awning of palmetto branches spread on a frame work of crotched uprights and cross sticks.

The health of the men improved rapidly. Their life was rather monotonous—drill, dress parades, reviews by Major-General Hunter and guard mountings taking up the time. The enemy was not near us, the labyrinth of rivers and waterways surrounding the nest of Islands known as Port Royal, enabling the light draught gunboats of the fleet to keep them on the inland, well out of our way.

Captain Stanwood of D had resigned before now, its First Sergeant, Brady, had been promoted to Second Lieutenant of Company G, and Second Lieutenant Butler, of Company H, was made First Lieutenant of D, and commanded the company.

The 4th day of April, the regiment, the 104th Pennsylvania, with General Naglee, Colonel Davis, and their staffs again reembarked on the old Cahawba, and the 5th sailed in a fleet for the North Edisto Inlet. Anchoring in that now crowded roadstead, we waited the success of the fleet's attack on Charleston, when the division was to land and march on that city. But the fleet found the forts guarding Charleston Harbor beyond their weight, so clearly so that as Admiral Ammen puts it, "even the common sailors knew that Charleston could not be taken without a protracted siege." The only thing left for us all to do, was to return to Port Royal, which we did the 10th of April, the old Cahawba leaving the swiftest of the fleet out of sight on the run, even sacrilegiously running by the "Flag Ship" of our transport squadron, and entering Port Royal while that seat of authority was still hull down.

It was our last cruise on the steamer Cahawba. Afflicted as it was with the third plague of Egypt, it had been our home for so many days, had borne us safely over such a stretch of water, in storm and calm, that we had a rough affection for the stout old transport ; and for Mr. Davis, her second mate, too. We had heard the command from the wheel-house so often of "Stand by your anchor, Mr. Davis," and the hoarse return of that old mariner, "Ay, ay, Sir," that he seemed part of the ship itself. As the regiment came alongside in a small steamer to go on board the Cahawba, to take a part in this very expedition, and our men saw the head of the rough old sailor peering over the side of the Cahawba at them, what a yell of "Stand by your anchor, Mr. Davis," rang out of five hundred throats. I am sorry to have to state that instead of the orthodox reply to this nautical command, Mr. Davis only growled "There's that damned Eleventh Maine again." The Cahawba steamed up the Sound to Beaufort with us the 11th of April, where the regiment landed and went into camp.

Lieutenant Butler, who had been ill for a day or so, now grew worse rapidly. His disease proved to be a malignant fever. He died April 14th. We buried him in the cemetery in Beaufort, with the military honors due his rank. His grave was near that of another young officer, one who had died in the Mexican war, and whose body had been brought home to be buried. I remember that over the young South Carolinian's grave stood a monument representing the trunk of a young palmetto tree, its top broken off. Where Butler is buried I do not know, at his old home, I hope ; and if he sleeps under the marble representation of a young, prematurely splintered pine tree, it is fitting. Young, handsome, intelligent, respected and admired by his men, cut down at his post in his years of high promise, wherever his grave is, it is that of a true son of our old Pine Tree State.

Our sojourn at Beaufort was a pleasant one. The town, though now sadly neglected, retained all its beauty of semi-tropical flowers and plants, and, under a beautiful sky, in an enervating climate, we took lazy comfort in our camp on the bank of the river. Besides a plentiful supply of regular rations, the men of D were here regaled with lucious blackberries. They grew abundantly in the neighborhood, and the negroes were delighted to exchange quantities of them for our broken victuals. We had a big Quartermaster's "fly" pitched for our company and a long table built down the center of the space it covered, with benches fitted on each side of it. And when the table was set for breakfast with bright tin dishes—the men's plates and cups—with a ration of good white bread by each plate that our own Prince Dunifer had baked for us at the post bakery, with hot coffee in the cups, and mess-pans filled with baked beans strewed along it, that table was a sight for a hungry soldier. And at dinner, with boiled beef and rice in place of the beans, it looked appetizing enough, too But at supper, with tea in place of the coffee, and with each plate well filled with ripe blackberries to eat with the white bread, and with dishes of brown army sugar to pass around among the sweet-toothed, it bordered on the luxurious. But where was the soldier that was ever satisfied with his rations? Not in Company D, anyway. Under the leadership of one or two past masters in the art, the men growled at even these rations until the cooks threatened to reduce themselves to the ranks. This would not do. The Articles of War didn't seem to cover the case, providing neither shooting nor hanging for this particular offense. When, lo, some one in authority had a bright thought. It was adopted, the cooks returned to the ranks, and the leaders in the grumbling mutiny, somewhat aghast, found themselves in charge of the cook house. They were told that such excellent critics of cookery must needs be good cooks, but the argument didn't hold good, though seemingly logical, for they proved not to be good cooks; nay, they were the worst ones D ever had. The men tried to swallow their discontent from very shame, but they could not swallow the victuals. The discontent became an uproar, with the result that the old cooks returned to the cook house, and if the men of D grumbled thereafter beyond the wide latitude military custom allows, they took good care to do so, as Corporal Annis used to smoke, with their heads under their blankets.

FERNANDINA, FLORIDA.

The fourth day of June the Eleventh went on board the steamer Boston and sailed for Fernandina, Fla., to relieve the 7th New Hampshire.

Fernandina, a city of two or three thousand inhabitants, is situated on the Cumberland Sound side of Amelia Island, a large island off the Florida coast particularly, though from Fernandina in sight of a southeastern bit of the State of Georgia.

For four months we garrisoned Amelia Island; those of the Eleventh that did not go from there to Morris Island with Lieutenant Sellmer of D, who took a detachment made up of men from Companies C, E, G and K, to the seige of Charleston, they manning the famous Swamp Angel battery. We that were left behind at Fernandina, excepting Companies A, stationed at the Railroad Bridge, and C, garrisoning Fort Clinch at the mouth of the harbor, were languidly occupied for these four months with our camp and picket duties, the picket one being the only duty at all arduous. This picket service was entirely confined to guarding the railroad that comes into Fernandina from across a bridgeable point of the sound. In fact, this was the only way the enemy could get at us except by boats, the road running through a series of the swamps, the south half of Amelia Island seeming to be formed of hummocks of comparatively dry ground. It was on some of these hummocks that our picket posts were stationed, on rises of ground in the middle of alligator and snake-invested swamps, where a breed of the most sanguinary mosquitoes imaginable filled the air at night to an extent that not only made it impossible for a man to sleep, but forced him to keep his already net-covered head in a thick smudge of smoke.

Admiral Ammen says that Amelia Island contributed so little to the purpose of the Confederates, that, though they fought for Port Royal, they made us a present of Amelia Island, evacuating it so thoroughly, Fort Clinch and all, that but a few rifle shots were fired from thickets on the fleet that captured it. Still, whether from pride or wholesome military caution I know not, still our commander would have it that we occupied a post of extreme danger, and that we were liable to be surprised and overwhelmed by a superior force at any time. And one night for some reason yet unknown to me, there came a general alarm, routing out all of our little army, even the peaceful camp guard being aroused from its slumbers and its sergeant ordered to fall his men in and follow the commander of the post. The commander led us to the road that runs from Fernandina to Old Town (once *the* Fernandina itself), near Fort Clinch, and we followed him into the swamp that lies between the old and the new towns, a swamp that is an impassable jungle of trees and tangled grape vines, the haunt of alligators and snakes and the breeding place of the most blood-thirsty breed of mosquitoes I ever had fasten upon me, led us down into the head of the narrow corduroy road running across this swamp, and bade us stand there and hold the pass at all hazards, for all I now remember throwing out a few encouraging words about the fame of Thermopyle and the Immortal Three Hundred, then turned and rode away towards Fernandina, with his orderly dangling at his heels, leaving us in the midst of a dense and ever-thickening cloud of bayonet-billed mosquitoes.

The enemy? Suppose he was to land at Old Town, take Fort Clinch, and put Captain Nickels and its garrison to the sword, must we stand there and be eaten alive for a little thing like that? Not if we knew it. We forthwith resolved ourselves into a council of war, with the result that we marched ourselves to the high·land overlooking the swamp, where the night breeze swept the pursuing mosquitoes back into their haunts. Then, after stationing a guard between us and Fernandina to prevent our alert commander from surprising us, we went into bivouac, confident that our danger did not lie towards Fort Clinch, for neither loyal nor rebel was yet so desperate as to tread that stretch of mosquito, alligator, snake-infested swamp road in the darkness of a moonless night. After some weeks spent on this, then isolated island, where a mail steamer from Port Royal put in only about once in three weeks, and no other vessel, except the gunboat cruising on the Cumberland Sound station, ever put in except when forced to by an extraordinary Atlantic gale, the Eleventh was relieved by the 97th Pennsylvania, and October 6th went on board the Boston again to proceed to Morris Island, that it might take part in the seige of Charleston.

MORRIS ISLAND.

Morris Island is but a strip of white sand on the Atlantic Ocean, at the mouth of Charleston Harbor. It runs north and south nearly, and is about four miles long. Its broad southerly end lying well out of the range of the enemy's fire, served as a camp-ground for troops not actively engaged in the siege and for headquarter and depot purposes. Narrowing as it approaches Sumter, till Fort Wagner completely barred all further progress at fairly high water, the island ends in a hooked projection known as Cummings' Point. It was on this point that Beauregard built Battery Gregg as long ago as when Sumter was forlornly garrisoned by Major Anderson.

From Cummings' Point it is but 1300 yards to Sumter, due northwest, and but four miles to Charleston City, looking about directly west across the bay, and is but about a mile and a half across to the batteries on Sullivan's Island, where Moultrie and its batteries lay beyond Sumter and to its east Sullivan's Island running about east for a short distance and then bearing rapidly towards the northeast, the north end of Morris pointing to about the western end of Sullivan's. To the west of the upper part of Morris Island, across a marshy tideway, through which flows Vincent Creek, James Island points a blunt end to Morris, the length of James forming the southern boundary line of Charleston Harbor. Outside of James, on the Atlantic, and separated from James by the Stono River, lies Folly Island, with Black Island wedged in between Folly, James and Morris.

When we reached Morris Island the tragedy of the siege was over, the whole of the island was in Union possession, and Wagner and Gregg were being rebuilt from the wreck occasioned by the terrible bombardment they had undergone, were being turned and armed to operate on the enemy's batteries on James and Sullivan's Islands, Sumter standing no longer as the chief, though still as an important factor in the problem of getting into Charleston, it having been battered from its aggresive symmetry into a silent, crumbling ruin. But from something like sentimental reasons it was still considered the central point of offense and defense, the rebel flag still flying defiantly over its ruined bastions, the garrison burrowing in bomb proofs that every shrieking shell of ours but added to the strength of, crumbling and tumbling the broken stone work in yet deeper depths above them. From these burrows they watched for night sallies from shore and fleet, and by the aid of the enfilading fire of the guns of James and Sullivan's Islands, succeeded in beating all off that were made upon them.

As the fatigue parties worked with shovel and spade in the sand of Fort Wagner and of Battery Gregg, the lookouts on the parapets would see a round cloud of white smoke fly into the air, from James Island perhaps. Then, with a cry of "James Island," they would leap from the parapets to cover, while the busy shovelers would scatter for shelter, instinctively taking cover under the sand walls next James Island till the projectile, shot or shell, from gun or mortar, had exploded and the fragments had buried themselves deep in the sand. Or, the cry might be "Sullivan," then the cover was sought for under the sand walls next that island. As soon as the danger was over, all rushed back to their work again. But sometimes this enfilading fire would become so vigorous a one as to force the men to quit work for a time and take shelter in the great bomb proofs and magazines, built of squared logs, banked and heaped with such depths of sand that even the fifteen-inch shells of the ironclads has failed to make any impression on them during their bombardment. All this time our own batteries on Morris Island were keeping up a steady fire upon Sumter and the other rebel fortifications, the fleet taking advantage of good weather to leave their stations outside the rebel line of fire to steam in and join in the roaring chorus.

Our regiment was encamped in the shelter of some sand hills about half way down the island. From this camp details of men for fatigue duty were sent to the upper part of the island to take part in the fortification building going on there, D men with the rest. But in a short time a number of D were detailed to serve as artillerymen in Battery Chatfield, a work on Cummings' Point, and so many of D were in this detail that it may be said that the Company was on artillery service in the mortar battery of Chatfield, where, under Lieutenant Sellmer's practical tuition, they soon became able heavy artillerymen. The men of C, E, G and K, who had served with Lieutenant Sellmer in the Swamp Angel Battery, were in this detail also.

Our battery work was mainly directed against ruined Sumter. Day after day we trained the mortars on that crumbling fortress, sending their ten-inch shells high in the air to drop into Sumter and burst there. After a shot was fired it was watched by Lieutenant Sellmer through glasses, and its effect noted, whether it fell into the fort or outside of it, whether it burst in the air or after striking its objective point, the men at work in the magazine filling the flannel bags each charge of powder weighed out was enclosed in, receiving orders to put in more or less powder as the Lieutenant noted the effects of the shots, and those cutting the fuses receiving their orders to cut them shorter or longer from the same observations. As Lieutenant Sellmer observed the effects of the shots, Lieutenant Charles H. Foster of Company K, detailed to assist Lieutenant Sellmer, as he had in the Swamp Angel Battery, would note on a prepared form the results given him by Lieutenant Sellmer, so keeping a tabulated statement of each day's work during its progress, the number of shots fired and their individual results.

Sometimes these results were plain to all of us. A shot would fall into the fort and a whirl of flying fragments of stone or a leaping barbette caisson would tell us just where it had struck, and just what its effect was, and a few times we succeeded in our unceasing endeavor to bowl the rebel flag down. But to the credit of the garrison of Sumter, it must be said, that no sooner was it down than some brave fellow would mount to the parapet and set it flying again.

There is rarely any great loss of life through artillery firing. While the singing of minie balls has an ominous sound in the ears of the most hardened veteran, the roar of a battery, except at close quarters, when throwing grape and canister, is not very alarming to him. Why, at the great artillery duel of White Oak Swamp, in June, 1862, our loss, except in artillerymen, was slight, and the artillerymen killed and wounded were mostly picked off by the rebel sharpshooters, while General "Dick" Taylor, who commanded the Confederate troops immediately across the bridge, says that severe as was our fire, their loss from shells was but a small one. So, in all the wild uproar at the siege of Charleston, our loss from flying shells was ridiculously small, viewed from the standpoint of infantry engagements, the careful watch the outlooks kept from the parapets, the facility for shelter, and the promptness of the men in getting into safe places, saving many lives and limbs. But there were several narrow escapes, and some curious ones too. How shall we account for that of Lieutenant Foster, who after remaining comfortably seated for hours upon an empty ammunition box on the parapet of Chatfield, entirely ignoring the fast coming shots of the enemy, suddenly rose and stepped off the parapet, and just as he stepped off it, the box he had been seated on went into the air, struck by a piece of shell ! And that of Private Darling, who, working at a mortar, suddenly stepped backwards just in time to save himself from. being cut in two by the whistling copper bottom of a Brooks' rifle shell that went flying right across the spot he had just stood on. But it was not all so bloodless. One day, the 8th of December, a mortar shell struck the magazine of Chatfield in its weakest spot, and went crashing into it. For a moment we outside the magazine were panic stricken, expecting the immediate bursting of the shell and the blowing up of the magazine, in which we had many barrels of powder stored. But fortunately the shell was so surrounded with the tons of sand that poured into the magazine with it, that its bursting flame was completely smothered and did not touch a grain of our powder. We hastened to dig our buried men out, and found Corporal Albee, of C, killed by a piece of the shell, Private Kimball, of E, mortally wounded, and Sergeant Howard, of K, Corporal Bearce and Privates Maddox and Bragdon, of D, more or less severely injured.

We worked at our batteries during the day only, as a rule, returning to the regimental camp each night, leaving the batteries to be defended from any attempt of the enemy to occupy them by the heavy and light guns of direct fire, and by the infantry force that was marched up the island each night and ensconced in the bomb proofs of Wagner and Gregg. But such an attack never came, the Confederates contenting themselves with long range demonstrations, though frequently indulging in a heavy night shelling of our works, as if to cover a landing.

At these times the air would be full of artillery pyrotechnics, the flaring of bursting shells, and the sparkling arcs of mortar shells with their flaming fuses, described by an old writer as appearing in the night to be "fiery meteors with flaming tails, most beautifully brilliant." A fine exhibition for those out of range.

In December, reenlistments began from among the original men of the regiment, though they had a year yet to serve, proving to us that the government had settled down into the conviction that the war was far from being near its end. Many of D put their names on the reenlistment roll.

Later on, the 23d of January, 1864, D, with B, entered Fort Wagner as part of its garrison. It was really a sort of going into winter quarters—without the winter—for you could lie out of doors, under one blanket, in the nights of December and January, and sleep as comfortably as a soldier need to.

The siege of Charleston was really abandoned by now, and the troops that had been engaged in it were only held in hand until the time should come for them to go to Virginia to engage in graver operations.

Though regularly trained to use the thirty-two and the one-hundred pound Parrot guns Wagner was mainly armed with, we did not fire them often now except for range practice, or to send a shell now and then shrieking into Charleston. We usually aimed at the tall white steeple of St. Michael's Church, the most prominent object in the foreground of the city, and a most useful one to the Confederates, for a bright light kept burning at night from this steeple served as a guide to blockade runners. Getting the light within a certain range of one on Sumter and they could keep the channel and glide safely into the harbor. Not always, though. Early one foggy morning, that of February 2d, just after daybreak, a sentry called the attention of the sergeant of the guard to a patch of harder color in the soft atmospheric gray of the fog bank that lay between us and Sullivan's Island. A hasty inspection and a sudden lift of the fog showed us that there was a blockade runner fast ashore under Moultrie.

The alarm was quickly given, and in a few minutes a hundred-pound shell was whirling through the fog at the grounded blockade runner, the powerful impact of the shell serving to lift the fog enough to show us the lead colored vessel, with hundreds of men swarming in and out of it, engaged in a desperate attempt to unload freight before the Yankees should discover her presence. There was a wild scattering at the sound of the coming shell, the runner was left to serve us as a target, and we sent shell after shell into her until she was but a wreck.

Our Confederate friends would still favor us with a serenade of shot and shell in spite of our peaceful demeanor. And once or twice they did this so vigorously as to cause the commanding general to think they were really on the point of attacking us with infantry. Beauregard says that he made one of these night bombardments to give our commander just that idea to cover his own withdrawal of troops to Florida to General Finegan, about the time the battle of Olustee was fought in that state. Regiments of our troops would then come to Wagner to stand at the parapets all night, while we artillerymen worked the guns to keep down the enemy's fire. It was in one of these bombardments, that of Christmas night, that Private Laffin, of D, was so badly wounded, a piece of shell striking the bayonets of some stacked rifles, one of the pieces of shattered steel penetrating a leg.

This night our gunners paid particular attention to Charleston, I remember, throwing shells into that city until a large fire broke out in it, and then throwing shells at the glare of the fire. The men fighting the fire in the city, largely colored non-combatants probably, would succeed in getting the flames somewhat under control. We could see them lower and lessen, then they would suddenly flare up bright and red again, telling us that the screech of one of our going shells had driven the fire fighters to cover.

A "cruel war" it was, especially to non-combatants that circumstances of situation or greed placed in dangerous positions. Just think of the terror the enterprising sutler must have been in who had pitched a big tent outside of Fort Wagner that none of our boys having money need go without such delicacies as pickled pig's feet, canned condensed milk, ginger cakes, strong butter and slabby skim milk cheese, just think of the terror he must have been in when he would leave all these precious goods to destruction for the sake of his unexpectedly endangered person.

For a few days after his arrival he did a thriving business, then came one of the nights of heavy bombardment from James and Sullivan'sIslands. In the morning the tent was still on the beach, but with certain suggestive looking holes in it. An investigation showed a medley of goods shattered and piled into a chaotic mass by invading shells, but the sutler was not to be found. He did not appear to us again, but it was said that he evacuated his bed and fled to the lower extremity of the island, as the first shell broke unceremoniously in upon his private apartment. That afternoon men came with an army wagon and carried away what Lieutenant Nel Norris would call the "debris" of boxes and barrels with what little remained of the stock of goods. That there was little besides shattered boxes and barrels to cart away, may be somewhat due to the fact that the men of D and B had been busily engaged during the forenoon in buying goods in the absence of their frightened owner.

At last the time came for leaving Morris Island. The reenlisted men had gone away on their veteran furlough, and finally D and B rejoined the regiment, which had been camping on Black Island since early in February. The Eleventh proceeded to Hilton Head, from where it sailed away with other troops the 21st day of April for a point on the York River, Virginia, from where our fleet had sailed a little more than a year before for the purpose of capturing Charleston. That the attempt had been a failure is to be attributed largely perhaps to the route of approach chosen. Beauregard says that there were three routes of attack from the sea, and that Morris Island was the worst of the three. He says that had we effected a lodgment on James Island instead, and have overcome the garrison there, as we did that of Morris Island, we had but to erect batteries within such easy distance of Charleston as to make it untenable, and as we would also be in the rear of their outer line of defense, they would have been obliged to evacuate Sumter, Moultrie and Wagner, and give up the city. That a similarly successful descent upon Sullivan's Island would have given the control of the inner harbor to the fire of our ironclads, with a similar result. But that when we had Morris Island, our occupation of it neither involved the evacuation of Sumter and the other forts, the destruction of the city by a direct fire, nor the control of Confederate movements in the inner harbor by the ironclad fleet. Be this as it may, beyond the destruction of Sumter, and the taking of Wagner, little had been accomplished, and we left Charleston and its defenses much as we had found them, the fleet riding outside the bar, the rebel flags still flying over Sumter, Sullivan's and James, Charleston still in the distance, now as exultantly defiant as it had been sullenly so in the height of the siege.

THE CAMPAIGN OF 1864.

The regiment arrived at Yorktown, Va., April 24th, and landing at Gloucester Point, on the opposite bank of the York River, went into camp. Here the reenlisted men rejoined the regiment from "veteran" furlough, bringing with them 176 stalwart recruits. These new recruits were distributed through the companies, and though almost without drill or preliminary discipline, they marched, fought, bled and died in the rough campaign of '64 as manfully as did the seasoned veterans they strove in their pride to emulate, both in bravery and endurance.

Yorktown was a very familiar spot to most of us. It stood just across the

York River from our camp, on a high bluff-like shore, and still surrounded by the earthworks captured from Magruder, turned and strengthened by ourselves ; grass-grown in the months that had passed since we sailed away from them.

The plains below the town, where the camps of our brigade had been, were now white with the tents of a part of the troops of the newly organized army of the James. This new military organization was composed of the Tenth Corps, drawn from the troops in South Carolina, consisting of three divisions, commanded by Generals Terry, Turner and Ames ; the Eighteenth Corps of three divisions too, commanded by Generals Brooks, Weitzel and Hinks ; and of a cavalry division commanded by General Kautz. These corps were commanded respectively by Major-Generals Q. A. Gillmore and W. F. "Baldy" Smith, the whole army by Major-General Benjamin F. Butler.

Our regiment was in the Third Brigade of Terry's Division. The other regiments of the brigade were the 24th Massachusetts, 10th Connecticut, and the 100th New York.

BERMUDA HUNDRED.

On the night of the 4th of May the transports the army had embarked on set sail for Fortress Monroe, and on the 5th moved up the James River, reaching Bermuda Hundred the afternoon of the 5th, and by morning of the 6th had disembarked. Bermuda Hundred is a peninsula, made by a sweep of the James River to the east and by its tributary, the Appomattox. It is at the mouth of the latter river, on its north bank, City Point lying opposite it on the south bank. Petersburgh is twelve miles up the Appomattox on its south bank, and Richmond twenty-three miles north of Petersburgh, directly connected by a railroad and turnpike.

On the morning of the 6th of May our disembarked forces advanced to the neck of the peninsula, about six miles from the landing. This neck is here about three miles across from river to river, two miles and a half beyond our halting point the railroad runs, the pike running between. The ground we took up was superficially intrenched at first, the plan not looking to a protracted stay there, but to an advance on the railroad and pike, the taking of Petersburgh and a march on Richmond and its southern communications The force ready to oppose us was a small one, no larger than our brigade, and our army numbered some 30,000 men. But before vigorous steps were taken to capture Petersburgh, it had been reinforced by troops hurried forward from North Carolina by General Beauregard, our old opponent of the Department of the South, now in command of the Department of North Carolina and Southern Virginia. It was the head of this reinforcing column that successfully held Port Walthall Junction the 7th of May against a portion of our army. On the 9th we moved out to the front and destroyed the railroad between Swift Creek and Chester Station, a length of about six miles. On the 10th, the Confederate General, Ransom attacked this outlying force, but was repulsed. On the 12th we moved towards Richmond, Smith's corps on the right and ours on the left. We did not meet with any serious resistance this day. At night our line camped on Proctor's Creek. On the 14th we meet with more resistance. Smith found the works in his front too strong to be assaulted, but our corps moving to turn the enemy's right, resting on Wooldridge Hill, succeeding in forcing them to abandon their position there, and by night of the 15th we had driven them out of their whole outer line and into their interior one, and we were in position before Drury Bluff. But while we had been moving so slowly, Beauregard had been acting with such rapidity that he was now in the Drury's Bluff intrenchments with an army gathered from North Carolina and Richmond, and felt so strong that on the morning of the 16th he assumed the offensive, attacking Smith's right flank in the early morning, and capturing General Heckman and some hundreds of his brigade. Beauregard's plan miscarried somewhat, or he might have ended the career of the army of the James before it had fairly begun. He intended to get around our flank, while General Whiting should move out from Petersburgh with 5,000 men and attack our rear. His attack against Heckman was successful, but the other attacks on Smith's line failed, though the rebels captured four pieces of artillery, but his attacks on the line of our corps were all repulsed. Still we were pressed back, partly by the numerical force thrown against us and partly from our anxiety to cover our trains and keep our connections with Bermuda Hundred, where we had left but a small force. By night our army had given back until the rebels occupied their whole outer line again, but Whiting's force failing to advance, Beauregard could not press his advantage as he wished to, and before morning our whole force was safely behind the Bermuda Hundred intrenchments. The truth is that General Whiting was not a prohibitionist by any means, and this day of all days in his military career, he chose to exemplify that fact by getting drunk. Colonel Logan, of General Beauregard's staff, who took General Whiting written orders to move out the morning of the 16th, delivered them to him the night of the 15th, and was with General Whiting when on the morning of the 16th, beginning at daylight, he made his advance. Striking the Union picket line, his force was placed in line of battle, but made no advance during the day, in spite of Colonel Logan's expostulations and those of General D. H. Hill, "spending the day in arranging and rearranging his line," according to Colonel Logan, who does not doubt but had General Whiting followed his instructions the result would have been the capture of the entire force of General Butler.

Company D had not yet been actively engaged. It had been under fire a number of times though, quite enough to show the good stuff its new men were made of. It had taken an active part in tearing up the railroad, and had done a little long range skirmishing in which its only casualty was Private Annis, wounded on the 14th; but I think that the members of it who had been in the most serious danger were those on the picket line the night of the 13th.

The picket line of this night was in charge of Captain Mudgett. In running it he placed some of us before the open grounds in which stood the house before which Lieutenant Brannen, of Company I, was killed, and then by some devious piloting placed another line between us and our line of battle, a bit of duplication that was decidedly unpleasant to us of the outer picket line, for the Confederates were terribly uneasy that night, firing heavily all along their apparently very strong picket line, we replying, of course, but—*zip, zip*, in front of us was all very well, but where did the bullets that flew around us from the rear come from? The unpleasant fact speedily dawned on us that a picket line lay behind us firing too at the Confederate rifle flashes, as they supposed, but really at our own, so that we poor fellows were between two fires. To attempt to go back to expostulate with the pickets behind us was impossible, for the inevitable crashing through the underbrush between us and them would concentrate sure death upon the messenger. So all we could do then was to stay where we were, cease firing, and lay low. This last we did literally, lying flat on the ground while the bullets zipped viciously back and forth over us, one every now and then striking this or that side of a tree with a suggestive spat.

But Private Day would fire, to lie still and be shot at was contrary to his nature. Every once in a while his gun would bang from his position on the left of the line, giving the enemy in front and the line behind us a range by which to pelt us most dangerously. Again and again I had to go down the line and expostulate with John, but it was of no use, and at last I was forced to take my position with him and by sheer ill-temper keep him repressed, while he foamed with wrath at the idea of being compelled to lie still and silent to be shot at.

The night of the 15th our regiment took a position on the extreme left, where we threw up a sort of intrenchment in anticipation of an attack. But in the morning the heavy firing and the shouting told us that the other flank was the one attacked. We remained in our position a short time in the thick fog, hastily getting coffee boiling and the inner man strengthened for what seemed to be a coming day's work. Soon an order came for us to move to a position in support of the assailed line. As we moved rapidly along the line, we passed General Terry's headquarters, a small house, out of which the General rushed in his shirt-sleeves to admonish us to double quick "for God's sake." Then, striking a panting gait, we soon took position under a heavy fire.

Here we lay watching the give-and-take going on in front of us, expecting each minute to be obliged to fill a gap, but instead we were suddenly ordered to march rapidly to the rear and push down the pike toward Petersburgh till we should meet the supposed to be approaching Whiting.

And we did march rapidly. The fog was long gone, and the sun was beating down hot and strong. Men fell right and left, not bullet struck, but sun-struck. Caps were filled with green leaves, handkerchiefs were soaked in water and tied around swelling temples, but still it was "Forward," "Forward." The desperate pace seemed endless, but at last we were halted, formed in a strong skirmish line, and moved through woods till we reached a creek where we awaited the Confederate advance.

We could hear them talking and moving beyond the creek, but for reasons now known to you, they did not cross it. We remained in this position until night, then by a circuitous route, down one ravine and up another, under the piloting of Lieutenant Newcomb and Sergeant Payne we stole away, and soon found ourselves behind the outworks of Bermuda Hundred.

The 17th of May was passed by the men in necessary recuperation, and by the commanding officers in a rearrangement of lines, now looking to defense. That night the pickets at Warebottom Church reported a movement down the pike. The sound of trampling horses and the rattling of heavy wagons came clearly to their ears. It was conjectured that a wagon train was moving down the pike from Richmond to Petersburgh, and it was determined to attack it. Troops were hurried from the inner lines to the front, and the Eleventh was formed in line of battle and moved through the woods toward the pike. As it was a bright moonlight night, and the woods were fairly clear of underbrush, this movement was rapidly made, but suddenly, click, click, all along in front came the sound of cocking guns, and as our men threw themselves upon the ground, a crash of musketry came from a line of battle the Eleventh had almost run into. For an hour fierce firing was kept up by both sides, a battery of artillery on ours, placed near the church, adding not a little to the uproar by throwing shells over our heads. At last, when our ammunition had become exhausted, and while the men, their blood up, where clamoring for a fresh supply, orders came to fall back.

The wagon train proved to be Beauregard's trains and batteries moving down from Richmond, and well sheltered from us by a strong line of battle.

Of D, Private Carver received a severe flesh wound in this affair and Private George L. Butler was mortally wounded, the loss of the regiment numbering 26 men.

The 20th of May the enemy made a most determined but entirely unsuccessful attack on our outer line. We were not engaged, however. It was this day that the rebel General Walker was wounded and captured.

Only heavy skirmishing took place for some days after this, the night firing between pickets being especially continuous. During this comparative lull, and accounting for it partly, the enemy was building the Howlett House line, extending from the Howlett House Hill on the James to the Appomattox, by this line of intrenchments effecting the famous "bottling up process," and most effectually protecting their lines of communication between Richmond and Petersburgh.

As soon as General Grant learned of the futile result of Butler's movement, from which he had hoped so much, the destruction of Confederate communication with North Carolina, the investment of Richmond, and the consequent withdrawal of a large body of Lee's army from his own front, he directed that all the troops not actually needed to hold Bermuda Hundred be sent to him under command of General Smith. In consequence of this order, 16,000 of our army with 16 guns embarked the night of the 28th, and the 29th sailed for White House Landing on the York River, leaving a force of about 15,000 infantry and cavalry in the Bermuda Hundred intrenchments.

At about the same time General Lee ordered Beauregard to send him all the men he, too, could spare, which he did, retaining about 12,000 infantry and cavalry. There seems to have been a desire on the part of General Lee that still more of Beauregard's force be sent to him; even that Beauregard himself should go to him with all his available troops and take command of the right wing of Lee's army, leaving Petersburgh with a small force to take care of itself. But Beauregard was tenacious in his determination to hold his position on the south side of the James, and to keep his lines of intrenchments strongly manned. He argued that Butler's force was still large enough to endanger Petersburgh, even against the force he had retained, and it was to test this theory that he made the reconnoissance in force on the 2d of June which proved so disastrous to Company D.

The regiment went on picket duty the evening of June 1st, D taking position at Warebottom Church. The pickets had by this time settled into a state of armed neutrality, the more venturesome of them even trading in coffee and tobacco. Private Bridges, of D, was especially active in this sort of barter. He frequently went across the strip of ground that lay between the picket lines to drive lively trades with the enemy for tobacco, which was scarce with us, bartering coffee therefor, which was scarce with them.

Private Bridges, "Old Turk" as he was called, was a character. A half surly look in his eyes, something like that in those of a half tamed steer, caused him to receive the bucolic nick-name. He had ideas of his own about guns ; the Springfield rifles we were armed with he despised. He wanted a gun that would carry a bullet to the spot he aimed at. Somewhere, at Gloucester Point I think, he got hold of a sporting rifle, a heavy, thick barrelled, strongly grooved piece, and then the bother was to get suitable ammunition for it, our cartridges being much too large for its bore. After a deal of wandering through camps, he secured, through a good-natured cavalryman, a suitable cartridge for his gun, a carbine cartridge that fitted it perfectly. With a stock of these in his cartridge box he was ready for the enemy. Of course the carrying of this gun had to be winked at by his officers, and when he went on inspection, parade or guard duty he had to borrow a despised Springfield rifle from some one off duty to appear with, giving rise to a lately heard of story of his carrying two guns.

This evening of the 1st of June, Corporal Weymouth made himself the medium of exchange between the pickets.

He went towards the rebel picket line in the early evening and was met by one of their number whom he arranged to meet at the same spot in the early morning for the exchange of goods agreed upon.

The night was a moonless one, I remember, for, as we were not allowed fires, or to light matches on the outposts, when we wanted to learn the time of night we had to catch a fire-fly and make him crawl across the face of a watch, that when he flashed we might catch the positions of the hands. In the early part of the night the rebel batteries opened on our lines, firing most vigorously for a time, but as we did not reply they ceased firing after about one hour. It is probable that it was Beauregard's purpose to aggravate our batteries into replying that he might gather an idea of their positions and the number of their guns.

Morning came at last and the daylight broke. As soon as the light was strong enough to see clearly, Lieutenant Maxfield made a tour along the line of D, from right to left. He found Corporal Weymouth wide awake and in readiness to go out to meet his rebel friend when he should appear coming over the rebel works,

"There he is, Corporal," said some one as a form darted over the rebel line. "But he has a gun in his hand," Weymouth answered, and sure enough

Lieutenant Maxfield saw that the man they were looking at had a gun in his hand, and that he was accompained by a long line of other gray clad men, reaching out from his right and left, all with guns in their hands, too, and all moving swiftly toward our works.

In a moment the Lieutenant had shouted the alarm to his men, and as the sharp word of command rang out, every man, were he asleep or awake, sprang to his feet, every gun was to a cheek, and a rapid and effective fire was opened upon the now swiftly approaching enemy. So sure and cool were our men, far from being surprised, that in less than a minute the long line of the enemy in front of D was gone, those of them not fallen back to cover, lying on the ground dead or dying, the not too desperately wounded slowly crawling for spots sheltered from our fire.

The new rifle of Private Bridges was especially effective that morning every shot from it seeming to tell. His usually half closed eyes were wide open now and sparkling with joy. As he fired he would peer after his flying shot, and "I have hit him," he would triumphantly shout, and then proceed to reload his rifle with cool care. We were jubilant, for we had beaten the enemy off, but we speedily found that the pickets on our left had not been so fortunate. We could see them falling hastily back, and then over the open space before us that we had just cleared of one rebel skirmish line, a heavier one came rushing.

We fell back to a reserve pit on the run, entering it pell mell. Here we found Captain Lawrence and his company, H, and at his command a smart fire was opened on the pursuing enemy, driving them to cover. But unfortunately there was an unoccupied reserve pit to our rear and left that the enemy entered, and from which they poured a galling fire on our rear. Captain Lawrence, as commander of our little force, was ably assisted by Lieutenant Thompson of his own company, and by Lieutenant Maxfield, of D. These officers exposed themselves recklessly while urging the men to keep up their fire on the enemy in their front, not forgetting those in the reserve pit behind us.

Of course we could not stay where we were unless we proposed to go to Richmond before its evacuation. A hasty council of war was held by the officers, and it was agreed that the plan should be to fight desperately until a lull in the attack should give an opportunity to gain the woods behind us, then that we should break for it with a sudden and combined rush that would carry us right through the enemy of the reserve pit should they sally out as we ran by them, which we must, and within a few feet of them. The rebels in our front made several vain rushes at us. Once a sergeant of theirs led his men almost to the muzzles of the guns on the left, at a moment too, when the most of the guns there were uncharged. Corporal Weymouth was on the extreme left, "shoot that sergeant, Weymouth," was shrieked at him, and like lightning Weymouth's gun was pointing straight at the gallant rebel, and Weymouth's sharp eye was looking down the barrel as if to give the death stroke. Even rebel human nature probably fighting for a commission could not stand it, and the sergeant turned and fled, his men flying with him, not knowing that Weymouth's gun was as empty as a last year's bird's nest.

A movement of the rebels in our front that checked the fire of their men in the reserve pit indicated a sudden onslaught. The moment for retiring had come, "now, all together," said Lieutenant Maxfield, as he ran along to the left, "pour it into them when Captain Lawrence shouts 'fire,' and then run for the woods," "Fire," the order came, a crash of rifles answered it, and then we ran like deer for the sheltering timber.

The enemy in the reserve pit was nonplused for a moment, for it looked as if we were charging straight upon them, but catching the idea in a moment they arose and poured a sharp fire into us as we ran by. Within a minute those of us not killed, made prisoners, or too badly wounded to be carried off the field, had rejoined the Eleventh, which we found in line of battle not many rods in rear of the scene of our desperate defence.

Of D, Private Bridges was killed in the reserve pit, Sergeant Brady, Corporal Bailey, Privates Conforth, Moses E. Sherman, Smith, Dawe, Dyer and Bragdon were wounded, Captain Mudgett, Sergeant Blake, Privates Bryant, Kelley and Bolton were prisoners, Private Bolton having been too badly wounded to be taken from the field. Of these prisoners all were eventually exchanged and discharged, except Private Kelly, who died in Andersonville Prison.

We find it reported that of Company H, Privates Cumner and Rogers were killed, and that Lieutenant Thompson and Private Green were wounded. The loss of the Regiment for the day was 41 in killed, wounded and prisoners. Lieutenant-Colonel Spofford, who was in command of the Regiment, was mortally wounded before the line was broken and the command then devolved on Captain Hill, of K, shortly Major and then Lieutenant-Colonel, and from this day on the most conspicuous commanding officer the Regiment ever had.

The picket skirmishing that had died out to a large extent during the last week in May, became continuous again from this attack of June 2d. Our own Regiment when not on the picket line engaged in this desultory sort of warfare, was lying in line of battle behind the heavy inner works of Bermuda Hundred, consisting of strong redans, or batteries, connected by infantry parapets, all with stout abbatis in front, and with slashings wherever possible, and from Beauregard's report, his men lay behind their somewhat similar works as anxiously as we did behind ours, both we and they in continual expectation of an assault. The truth is that both Butler and Beauregard were afraid that their long and thinly manned lines might be assaulted and carried at any moment, each knowing his own weakness full well, and magnifying the strength of his opponent.

Beauregard had the best ground for his fears. As the strongest numerically and occupying the inner and therefore the shorter lines of the opposing works, and with a strong fleet of gunboats in the river to fall back to the shelter of in case of disaster, the initiative belonged to us. And indeed a force did move out from our line the 9th of June to attack Petersburgh. General Gillmore with 3,000 infantry, accompained by General Kautz with 1,500 cavalry, crossed the Appomattox on the ponton bridge at Port Walthall in the early morning. Gillmore moved out on the City Point Road, and Kautz moved to the left four or five miles to reach the Jerusalem Plank Road. Gillmore finding the works before him strong ones, and apparently well manned, did not attempt to assault them, returning to Bermuda Hundred that afternoon. Kautz attacked on the plank road with indifferent success at first, but finally flanked the enemy's line, forcing them out of their ranks, then marched on the city, but reinforcements coming to the enemy and Gillmore not supporting him, Kautz was forced to withdraw. But more formidable opposing forces than were those of Butler and Beauregard, forces commanded perhaps by greater cheiftains than they, too, were now moving to the position of which Petersburgh was the central figure, now to become the most important position of the war.

Before the battle of Cold Harbor was fought by the Army of the Potomac and the portion of the Army of the James sent to Grant under General Smith, Grant had about given up all hope of breaking through Lee's defence on the north side of the James, and had planned, if this last effort failed, to move across the James to a position before Petersburgh, hoping to be able to move so unexpectedly to Lee as to effect the capture of Petersburgh, the turning of Beauregard's Bermuda Hundred line, and to cut off Confederate communication with North Carolina before Lee should realize Grant's object sufficiently to checkmate it by throwing the Army of Northern Virginia across the James and into the Confederate intrenchments at Bermuda Hundred and Petersburgh in time to save them. The part of the Army of the James under General Smith marched to White House, reembarked and sailed for Bermuda Hundred, arriving in the afternoon of June 14th. Smith's force crossed the Appomatox by the ponton bridge at Broadway Landing, two miles from Port Walthall and eight from Petersburgh. Assaulting the works they found in their front, they succeeded in carrying a long line of them. Divisions of the Army of the Potomac began to reach Smith's position that afternoon, crossing the James on a ponton bridge laid down from Wilcox Landing on the north side and Windmill Point on the south, just below City Point, but owing to the exhaustion of troops, missent orders, and various other causes, the success of the forenoon was not followed up, and the 16th and 17th were spent by our forces there in making assaults on the strong and, though mainly defended by artillery, still well defended rebel works. The results were varying during these two days, but without our gaining a position of sufficent strength to enable our columns to overcome the defence of the 18th, when Beauregard's small, almost exhausted and somewhat provisional army was heavily reenforced by Lee's veteran troops.

During this time we were holding the lines of Bermuda Hundred, in hourly expectation on the 16th and 17th of the Army of Northern Virginia assaulting us, it having to pass so near us in moving down the pike and the Richmond and Petersburgh to Beauregard's assistance, that it might easily hurl an assaulting column on our lines and breaking through the inadequate force with which we held them, assail Grant on the flank.

While Beauregard, thoroughly alive to Grant's real purposes through the stories of scouts and spies, and the sifted admissions of the prisoners he captured on the 15th, was showering telegrams on Lee and sending his aides with personal messages to Richmond, Lee was still on the north side of the James throwing out reconnoissances in every direction in search of Grant's real course. This delay of Lee forced Beauregard to hold his lines with a very small force against a constantly augmenting one. But these lines were formidable ones. A born engineer as well as an educated one, Beauregard had from sheer restlessness already entrenched every practicable position around Petersburgh, planting enfilading batteries on all commanding points, and generally had already planned and arranged the lines of works that, with little modification of position, held Petersburgh so long against our armies.

Knowing that the force in his front was steadily growing as divisions of the Army of the Potomac came on the ground and went into position, and that the 16th would be a day of trial to him, Beauregard the night of the 15th determined to abandon the Bermuda Hundred line, trusting to the coming of Lee's troops to regain them.

That night he withdrew the force that held the Bermuda Hundred lines, leaving only a mask of pickets, virtually abandoning his whole line from the Howlett House to the Appomattox. He says he had the guns and caissons of the Howlett House Battery removed and buried, the ground above them rearranged with sticks and leaves as not to arouse any suspicion, and that this prize remained safely hidden until the Confederates had regained their line.

The night of the 15th Lieutenant-Colonel Greely of the 10th Connecticut, which regiment was on picket at the Warebottom Church position, hearing movements on the rebel line, crept out and made up his mind from what he heard and saw that the rebels were moving away. Reporting his belief and his reasons for it to General Terry, that officer ordered a movement in the early morning of the 16th that resulted in the capture of the whole rebel line with their pickets and such troops as they had left there.

A force of one hundred day's men from Ohio had reported to General Butler, good material enough, but in the nature of things quite undisciplined, mere raw recruits, and without the veteran organization of officers and men that enabled our own new men to do such good work. These new troops were placed in the captured lines, while we held our own outer line just across the slashing dividing the two lines of intrenchments. They now held their position beautifully so long as they were not troubled by the Confederates, but along in the afternoon a commotion was visible among them, then a few came hurrying over the works they were in, then more and more, a confused firing was heard, then the "rebel yell" rose clear and shrill and the whole force of Ohio men came flocking over the works and across the slashing, a strong skirmish line of gray clothed soldiers moving after them—the van of Lee's army. The hundred day's men came tearing towards us at the top of their speed without order or orders so far as could be seen. We opened ranks to let them through, the scared white faced flock of sheep, one of them, I remember, holding up a hand from which the blood was trickling from a scratch probably made by a limb of a fallen tree of the slashing, lamentably crying "I'm wounded," "I'm wounded," while our men roared with laughter. What would have become of them—whether they would have stopped short of Ohio—I do not know, had not the 10th Connecticut, on reserve, deployed with fixed bayonets and fenced the mob back.

But we had no time for enjoyment of this part of the comedy. Closing up as the Ohio men passed through us, we turned so heavy a fire on the advancing lines of the enemy that they stopped, staggered, fell back and finally retired to their recaptured works.

At day-break of June 17th, General Osborn says that the Confederates assaulted the Union line in our front and were repulsed, but when they assaulted in the afternoon they broke through a portion of the line, driving it back.

Captain Maxfield's diary states that in the evening of the 17th, the Eleventh charged to support the left of the 24th Massachusetts, where some one-hundred day men had given way, our Ohio runaways again. It was in this charge that Corporal Bearce was wounded. And for the 18th this diary states that we had fallen back to the old line of rebel rifle pits, back of the church, and that either intentionally or by accident the rebels set fire to the recaptured church, and it was burnt to the ground.

The night of June 18th, after the corps of the Army of the Potomac had made a series of desperate and bloody assaults on the Confederate works at Petersburgh, works that military authorities agree should have been taken the 15th, could have been the 16th, might have been on the 17th, but that were impregnable for the time now that the lines of the Army of Northern Virginia were stretched behind them, General Grant, recognizing the futility of further direct efforts against Petersburgh, gave orders that all assaults should cease, and that the positions gained by the several corps close against the enemy's lines should be intrenched, and as General Humphreys says of the intrenchments threw up that night by this order, "the two opposing lines of works before Petersburgh remained substantially the same in position to the close of the war."

DEEP BOTTOM.

In the afternoon of the 20th of June, the Regiments of our brigade broke camp and marched to the James River, crossing it by ponton boats after dark, landing at Deep Bottom, on the north bank of Bailey's Creek, emptying into the James. The position so quietly taken was three miles east of the Howlett House Battery, and though four miles north of it by terra firma measurement, it was fifteen miles below it in the flow of the river, so crooked is the James at this point of its course. Deep Bottom was a well wooded bluff when we seized it, but 'twas bare enough before many days, so vigorously were axes plied by the men of our regiment, and while they were renewing their youth as axemen, fatigue parties from regiments more used to the spade were throwing up a strong line of works, batteries connected by infantry parapets and with outlying rifle pits, forming when completed and with gunboats anchored on the flanks, a practically impregnable "bridge head" for the ponton bridge now laid across from the south bank of the James to Deep Bottom.

We remained at Deep Bottom for several weeks, within easy reach of strong outlying works of the rebels, partly thrown up and strengthened after our arrival. Their main outer line on this side of the river, the Chapin's Bluff one, was about four miles northeast of Deep Bottom. The opposing lines at Deep Bottom were some distance apart, from half a mile to a mile, but portions of the picket lines were very near together, particularly in the extensive fields to the north of Deep Bottom. In the immediate front, looking east, there was a wide stretch of woods, a tongue of the woods that ran along both sides of Bailey's Creek from its wide mouth, a mouth of such uncommon depth as to give the position we held on its north shore the name of Deep Bottom. But without the animus of a momentarily expected attack, the picket of both sides were amicably disposed, meeting in a big corn patch in the open field to gather green corn and to barter. There used to be a story that some of them occasionally visited a secluded spot to indulge in friendly games of cards together, with coffee and tobacco for stakes.

An occurrence that will interest fatalists took place at Deep Bottom. A member of the 24th Massachusetts had deserted from that regiment to the enemy while the regiment was in North Carolina. It was undoubtedly his plan to take an early opportunity to desert from his new service to our lines again and get sent North out of the way of any possible casualty, for he took an early opportunity to get taken prisoner at Deep Bottom during one of our reconnoissances there, the Confederate regiment he had joined having been sent to Virginia and located before Deep Bottom. But, strange to say, the double deserter passed directly back into the arms of his old company of the 24th Massachusetts. A dramatic situation it must have been both to him and his old comrades. Recognized in a moment, he was imprisoned, tried and sentenced to be shot, and the sentence was carried out in the fields between our works and those of the Confederates.

Little of memorable moment took place for a time. Captain Maxfield's diary has these entries for the month following our arrival at Deep Bottom. For June 22d, that men of the 10th Connecticut had found a pot of gold. He does not record whether they did so at the end of a rainbow or not. For July 1st, that Brigadier General R. S. Foster took command of our brigade, and that Colonel Plaisted, who had been Brigade commander so far on the campaign, returned to the command of the Eleventh. For the 3d, that Captains Hill and Baldwin were mustered as Lieutenant-Colonel and Major respectively, and that Company A was sent across Bailey's Creek "to hold it." This entry argues a large liquid capacity for that company.

It was about this time that General Hill, then our Lieutenant-Colonel, had an adventure that would have been a misadventure but for his characteristic readiness. General Foster requested him to go out through the big corn field already told of, and learn what he could of the force of the rebels in our front, and to do it in his own way, having learned that as a daring, long-headed scout, General Hill was without a peer in our brigade. Taking a couple of orderlies with him, General Hill rode into the interior until he judged he was a mile from the river, not seeing any rebels yet, then he bore to the left to strike the river away above us, intending to ride down along the river bank to Deep Bottom. After riding for about a half mile towards the river, he suddenly rode into the rear of an undeployed rebel picket force of about twenty-five men. Clustering around him, their officer laughingly asked the General "where he was going." Personally the General felt very sure that he was going to Richmond, however much against his will, but putting on a bold face, he answered, "that he had rode out to get the news by exchanging papers with them." "This is pretty cool," said the rebel officer, "let me see your papers." Luckily the General had a copy of the *New York Tribune*, and one of the *Philadelphia Inquirer* in his pocket, and luckily too, a rebel sergeant here said "this is the same officer that sent us a paper the other day." This was so, the General, a week before, when officer of the day, having effected an exchange of papers with this sergeant through the medium of one of our men, when the sergeant must have taken a sharp look at the officer who moved so cooly along a dangerous picket line. "Well," said the good-natured rebel lieutenant, "I guess I will let you go, you look as though you were telling the truth. But I must say you took a good deal of pains to come so far, and to come in our rear, too." Our General with the guileless face answered "that he got lost in riding out, and was trying to find his way into camp when he rode up to them." Drifting into a general conversation with the officers and his men, each party covertly tried to learn a little something concerning the other's force on that side of the river, until the General, having learned all he wished to, embraced a good opportunity to make his adieus. As he rode away with his eager orderlies riding on his heels, the Confederate officer, on whom the real purpose of the General's mission had dawned, but who was too honorable to take back his given word, called out, "Remember this, you can't play at exchanging papers with me again." With this friendly warning from the "good fellow," as the General rightly calls him, ringing in their ears, the little Union party spurred its horses into a magnificent burst of speed that quickly took it out of all possible danger of having to obey a recall.

For July the 10th Captain Maxfield's diary states, that (among others) First Sergeant Bassett, of D, reported for duty from recruiting service in Maine, where he had been for some months. For the 12th, that an expedition from the 10th Connecticut went up the river and captured a lieutenant and fourteen men, besides burning a mill. For the 13th, that two prisoners were taken by a scouting party under Major Baldwin and Captain Nickels, and that some of D were in this party. Possibly it was this expedition that Private William Sherman, of D, shot the rebel "stone dead," as he declared, but while he was reloading his gun the supposed to be dead man jumped up and ran away regardless of Sherman's hilarious expostulations.

For the 14th, the diary states, that the rebels opened fire with a battery they had stationed in a ravine and that their shells killed "a horse and six men" on the gunboat Mendota. It would appear from this that there were veritable "horse marines" in our navy.

For the 21st, the diary states that our regiment moved across to Strawberry Plains, on the south bank of Bailey's Creek, and that we captured eleven prisoners, but that the enemy appeared in force and caused us to fall back into our intrenchments. For the 22d, that the regiment went to the Plains again, "we taking all we wished to," as the Captain modestly phrases it. For the 23d, that the regiment went to Strawberry Plains again, and met a strong force of the enemy, we losing two killed and four wounded, and that we remained that night on the ground we had taken during the day. For the 24th, that we were relieved by two regiments of the Nineteenth Corps, that Corps having just arrived from the Red River, and, by the way, its commander was our old brigade commander, General Emory. For the 25th, the diary tells us that the pickets of the Nineteenth

Corps on the Plains were driven in, and that we were ordered out to retake the position they had lost. For the 26th, that we were still skirmishing on Strawberry Plains in an effort to retake the lost position, and that by night, when we had recovered it, we had lost one man killed and twenty-one wounded, and that we were relieved by the Tenth Connecticut that night. For the 27th, that the Second Corps crossed to the Plains early in the morning.

These operations of our regiment on Strawberry Plains in the last days of July were in connection with a movement planned against the enemy's left flank, resting on our side of the James, and directly in our front.

After the assaults of the 18th of June, the immediate attempts of Grant to overcome Lee were confined to flanking movements from the right and left, north and south of the James. The plan of the movement we were initiating was that Hancock should move to Deep Bottom with the Second Corps and two divisions of cavalry under Sheridan, and that the Second Corps should try and break through the rebel line near Chapin's Bluff, at about the spot we operated in the following October ; then if the infantry succeeded in breaking the rebel line, the cavalry was to make a dash on Richmond, while Hancock should operate to prevent rebel reenforcements crossing from the south bank of the James by the ponton bridge they had laid down between Chapin's and Drury's Bluffs. And that if the dash on Richmond could not be made, then the railroad communications of the rebels on the north side should be destroyed as far as practicable. It was thought, too, that this movement, if unsuccessful in itself, might force the rebels to reinforce the north side so heavily as to cause such a reduction of their force holding the Petersburgh lines as to give a fair promise of success in the assault to be made when the mine in front of Burnside's Ninth Corps was sprung.

As a necessary preliminary to these movements, and to give the idea perhaps that the contemplated attack, which they could not help learning of the preparations for, through spies, prisoners and deserters, was a flanking one, by the way of Bailey's Creek, as, in fact, it finally became, the Eleventh crossed to Strawberry Plains, just on the other side of Bailey's Creek, having to cross the James twice to get there, once to the south side by the ponton bridge we held the head of, and then to the north side again by another ponton bridge laid down with its north side head debouching on the great cleared flat known as Strawberry Plains. Across the head of these Plains runs the River road, a connecting link of the system of roads leading into Richmond. Working our way up through the woods bordering Bailey's Creek, by night we had driven the enemy into his works guarding the road and outer lines, his main one lying on the Deep Bottom side of Bailey's Creek and running along that side of the Creek to Fussel's Mill at the head of the Creek, from which point his line was refused, as the military phrase is, that is it turned sharply back.

It was the position we had gained before this outer line that we turned over to the Nineteenth Corps and that they lost the 25th of July. The next day we pressed the enemy steadily back until we were lying close to their outer line, the gunboats firing sharply this day, throwing their heavy shells over our heads at the enemy's lines, the enemy replying as best they could with a battery of artillery they had brought down and stationed in the road. During the day a shell from a gunboat fell so unfortunately short as to fall just behind our right rifle pit, lightly scooped out pits, unconnected, each sheltering a half dozen men. It fell at just the most dangerous distance from our men, burst, and threw its fragments right among them, killing and wounding several.

During this night Hancock and Sheridan arrived with their troops. Halting their men on the other side of the river, they rode over to Deep Bottom and had a consultation with General Foster, who described to them what he had learned of the enemy's works in our front. Hancock then telegraphed to General Meade, his immediate superior, stating what had been told him, and doubting the advisability of assaulting so strong an intrenched line with the force at his command, and suggesting a flank movement by way of Strawberry Plains instead. General Meade coinciding with him in his opinon, Hancock moved his troops over the river to Strawberry Plains, and attacked soon after daylight on the 27th of July, the cavalry on his right.

General Miles moved to the front across the open field with a brigade in open order, charged and captured the enemy's battery, four 20-pound parrot guns, in a handsome manner. Then swinging to the right on its pivot, the position held by the Eleventh on the creek, the whole line moved out across the enemy's roads until it had invested his whole line, extending from our position on the creek to Fussell's Mill. The part of the infantry in the plan was now completed. The cavalry then proceeded to carry out the flanking operation it was charged with, but the rebels had been reinforced, four divisons of infantry and two of cavalry having come across the James and taken position in the works we were threatening, so that when Sheridan's cavalry moved out beyond Fussell's Mill they found the road barred by a heavy force of cavalry supported by infantry.

General Grant came across the river to the Plains that afternoon and made a personal observation of the rebel position, and deciding that not much could be done there, returned to his headquarters, from which he telegraphed General Meade that he did not wish Hancock to assault, but for him to hold his position for another day. For, though foiled in his attempt to make a dash on Richmond, Grant had learned that the reinforcements the rebels had hurried across the James had left their Petersburgh lines guarded by three infantry divisons only, while but one cavalry divison remained on that side of the river, and now hoped by threatening demonstrations to keep the rebel force on the north side, out of the way of the column he was already forming to assault the Petersburgh lines. In obedience to Grant's wishes, Hancock and Sheridan spent another day in holding the heavy rebel force far from the scene of Grant's new hopes, hurrying back to Petersburgh with their troops the night of the 29th, to take part in the assault that was to follow the mine explosion set for the morning of July 30th. The explosion took place as planned, but for various reasons the results were as disastrous to the Union as to the Confederate army. Returning to our camp at Deep Bottom, we spent a few days in comparative quietude, while a new movement in which we were to take part was in process of evolution.

General Grant had received information that General Lee was strongly reenforcing Early, now operating in the Valley, and believed the reenforcements were so largely taken from the troops on the north side of the James as to give a chance for a more successful operation on that side of the river than our late one had been. The troops to be engaged in this second attempt were largely those engaged in the first, the Second Corps, part of the Tenth, and a cavalry force under General Gregg, all to be under Hancock's command. But instead of marching directly across the river as before, Hancock's corps was to embark on transports at City Point and move down the river in the afternoon, to give the Confederate spies the idea that it was going to the Valley, but under the cover of the night the transports were to run back to Deep Bottom, the troops were to disembark at Strawberry Plains, move rapidly in the morning, turn the enemy's line on Bailey's Creek, and push for Richmond. But through lack of proper landing places the second corps was not disembarked until eight o'clock instead of at daybreak.

The part of the Tenth Corps men in the programme was that we were to assault in our front, which we did promptly at daybreak, the Second Corps' historian stating that we opened fire at five o'clock.

The Eleventh held the part of the picket lines running through the woods in front of Deep Bottom the night before the 14th of August. Though so far from the river we pickets had a suspicion that something was on foot. The ponton bridge crossing to Strawberry Plains was muffled, yet we could distinctly hear the rumble of the artillery and the tramping of the horses of Gregg's cavalry division as they crossed it, and the screeching of steamboat whistles was too continuous for secrecy too, though necessary from the darkness of the night and the crowding of so many boats in the narrow channel. If we heard it, and our suspicions were aroused by it, then our contiguous friends, the enemy, whose pickets could hear it all as well as we could, must have been forewarned of what was coming in the morning.

But we of the Eleventh had no idea that we were to take the sharp initiative that we did. In the early morning of the 14th Colonel Plaisted rode up to the reserve of D and directed Lieutenant Norris to deploy the reserve, move out to the picket line and advance with it until he met the enemy, then to press forward and capture his exterior lines. (Lieutenant Grafton Norris, of Company F, was in detailed command of D, Lieutenant Maxfield having gone North on an overdue leave of absence). The movement directed by the Colonel was immediately proceeded with, and in less time than it takes to tell it we had moved out, and our skirmish line was moving rapidly through the woods and was on the enemy's pickets. We forced them back on their reserve, stationed behind a strong line of rifle pits, with partly open ground before them immediately in front of D's skirmishers. This line ran along the top of the reverse side of a dip of the ground, covering a wood road that ran directly down this dip before crossing their line. As the men of D reached this road in hot pursuit of the enemy, its inviting smoothness led them to converge on it, and, frantic now with anticipation, to charge the enemy's works without orders. Lieutenant Norris and Sergeant Young saw the danger and tried hard to prevent this movement, rushing among the men to drive them out of the road, but before they had an appreciable time to enforce their commands in a withering rifle fire of the enemy swept the road, killing and wounding several of our men. In spite of this severe check the officers held their men close up to the enemy's works, on which we opened an eager fire. For a time our line was kept back by the enemy, but suddenly the exertions of our men were rewarded, the rebel line beyond our company's left giving way just as the enemy in our front had ceased firing ; and D took so quick an advantage of the opening that before the startled and momentarily confused enemy fairly knew what was happening we had mounted their works and were in possession of them.

We found that their slackened fire meant that they had not had their break-fasts any more than had we, and that they had relinquished firing in fancied security until they should have strengthened the inner man. Their untouched rations of freshly cooked bread, cooked in Dutch ovens after the peculiar South-ern style, with the side of fat bacon left behind them, satisfied the sharp monitions of several Yankee appetites.

The enemy had retreated to the main line, from which they opened a sharp artillery fire on us. This line across a wide field was so very formidable in appearance that an assault was not ordered.

Of D, Privates Hall, Shepard and Stanley had been killed, Corporals Keene, Weymouth and Privates Samuel A. Bragdon, Collins, Wm. Sherman, Adelbert Stratton and Alfred C. Butler had been wounded ; Weymouth mortally so. It is notable that Butler, an impetuous youth, fell close to the enemy's works, wounded in three places, and that his friend Bragdon received his mortal wound in a brave attempt to rescue him from his perilous position.

During the rest of the 14th we lay on the ground we had won, General Birney, our new Corps commander, having been ordered to suspend his opera-tions on account of the delay attending the movements of the second corps. It was a terribly hot day in open ground, General Mott reporting that of two small regiments of his Second Corps division exposed to it 105 men were prostrated by the heat.

This intense heat may have had something to do with the slowness and weakness of the Second Corps assault, for it was not delivered until four o'clock, and then with but one brigade, others intended for the attacking column having become too demoralized to make it wise to push them forward. The only effect of this movement was to draw enough of the enemy from our front to enable part of our corps to capture a battery of four eight-inch howitzers.

The record states the night of the 14th the greater part of our Corps was marched to the vicinity of Fussell's Mills at the head of Bailey's Creek, and that the order for the 15th was that our Corps should find the enemy's left and attack Gregg's Cavalry covering our flank, but that General Birney took so wide a circuit that it was night before he found the enemy's left and took position.

As for the Eleventh, we seem to have been placed on the left for the 15th, near the pivot, for we moved but little. The recollection is that we lay along a road most of the day, sheltering ourselves from falling rain in the bordering woods as best we could. At night we went into bivouac in a handsome grove of trees, and our wagons coming up to deal out company rations, D had a company supper, First Sergeant Bassett having arrived with the cooks and the men who, for one reason or another other than sickness, had been left in camp when we went on picket.

The morning of the 16th broke clear and cloudless, too cloudless, for it was soon evident that the 16th was to be a day like the 14th, when the men of the Second Corps suffered so terribly in men and morale. The regiment was on the move very early in the day. In moving for position we were soon under an aggravating fire, marching and counter-marching with men dropping out wounded or killed, until we took position in a dense wood where we were somewhat sheltered by a bend of ground. Here a column for attack was formed, the 1st Maryland Cavalry dismounted, serving as infantry and temporarily attached to our brigade, on our right.

Anticipating the coming assault, the enemy had thrown a heavy skirmish line into a line of rifle pits running along enfilading points, to sweep the woods with a galling fire. It is very unpleasant to lie in action under such a fire and see comrades to your right and left struck by unseen foes. If a man has nerves they are soon in a quiver, and if he has not known he had any before, he learns that he is not made quite of iron after all. We found it so in the half hour we lay in this position and it was really a relief when scudding aids dismounted and darting through the woods from tree to tree brought the order to charge. Quickly we arose to our feet, and rushed forward with the wild cry which seems as necessary to a charging force as the breath with which they give it. Almost immediately we were subjected to the most severe fire we were ever under. No mere skirmish line this, but an outlying line of battle. The woods fairly rang with the screeching of the bullets; still we pushed on, when suddenly the 1st Maryland fell back, not directly back, but obliquing into our own now swaying line, and in another second in spite of the shouts of their maddened officers, the men of the two regiments were falling back in confused mass.

But the men of the Eleventh were not at all panic stricken. Getting themselves out of the line of fire they turned voluntarily, and shaking themselves clear of the dismounted cavalry, closed up their shattered line. In a minute they were ready to go in again, and as General Foster rode on the scene, galloping along the line of his brigade to make sure that his regiments were making ready for another rush, and rode up to the Eleventh calling out " Forward, Boys," we dashed ahead, and before the enemy could repeat the withering tactics of a few minutes before, had driven them headlong from their rifle pits and were pursuing them to their main intrenchments under a heavy fire poured on us from their main line, which ran along a ridge of ground covered by a wide slashing of heavy bodied trees, felled in all directions. In charging through it the men were somewhat protected by the heavy logs, and fortunately, too, the enemy must fire down hill, giving a tendency to over shooting, else not so many of us as did would have reached the crest of the hill. Before we did, many had tumbled headlong among the fallen logs, and how any of us reached it, few can tell, but we did, the rebels retiring with more rapidity than grace as we poured into their works.

Beyond the captured line we found a smooth field of perhaps a hundred and fifty yards in width, dipping into a wood bordered run. It was to this run that the enemy had withdrawn, and from it they kept up a rapid fire on us, our men returning it with the more spirit that we had found boxes of cartridges strewed along the enemy's side of the works, cartridges that fitted our guns perfectly, so furnishing us with a much needed supply of ammunition.

But the fire that annoyed us most was an enfilading one from across a run beyond the left flank of our regiment. Beyond this run, on higher ground than we occupied, the enemy had built works to sweep the front of the works we had just taken. From here, snugly ensconced behind a difficult run, and hid from us by a stout growth of trees, left standing to mask their position, they swept our flank with a terrible fire. Efforts were made to dislodge them by sending brigades down our front to charge the run, but the cross-fire the charging brigades were subjected to forced them to retreat to cover. Suddenly fierce yells from the rebel lines announced that they were receiving reenforcements. The position was becoming serious.

As Colonel Hill and Major Baldwin had been badly wounded the command of the Regiment devolved on Captain Merrill of Company I. Our men were falling rapidly and those left were exhausted by the efforts they had made under a blazing sun, yet when a thin line of the Second Corps moved out of the woods behind us and advanced as if to support us in a charge we were to make by way of our left on the aggravating work on that flank, our men raised a glad hurrah and gathered their energies for a mighty rush. But, alas, the Second Corps men could not endure the murderous sweep of the fire the alert enemy poured upon them from their flanking position, and quickly melted back into the timber.

Movements in our front indicated a gathering of Confederates for an assault. Anticipating it somewhat, and its result, of which there could be but one, the colors of the regiments were sent to the rear, and the word was passed along the line that when broken the regiments were to rally at the line of rifle pits we had taken in the morning, where the men would find their colors planted. Then came the roar and rush of the assault, a minute of fierce firing and yelling, and we were flying back to the sheltering woods, a storm of bullets whistling around us.

A citizen seeing how badly we were broken, our men fleeing into the woods without apparant formation or visible control, would have sworn that none of us would have stopped short of the James River, but I don't believe that a man of ours anyway went back a foot further than the captured rifle pits. There we gathered on our colors, every man in his place, and as the enemy came dashing through the woods after a supposed-to-be flying foe they quickly learned what it was that Paddy gave the drum. Of D, Private Hanscom was killed this day, and Privates Day, Googing, Leighton, McGraw, Bubier and White were wounded.

While these operations were going on, Gregg's cavalry, supported by General Miles with a brigade from the Second Corps, had moved up the Charles City road, driving the enemy's cavalry before them, until our cavalry had reached White Tavern, only seven miles from Richmond. Reenforcements reaching the Confederate cavalry, Gregg was in turn forced back upon Miles, both finally falling back to Deep Creek, a tributary of Deep Run, fighting as

they retreated, holding one position until a portion of their men had taken a
second one a half mile or so back of their advance one, then the advance
line would fall back behind the new line and take up a position about half a mile
or so further in the rear in their turn, all this time carrying their dead and
wounded with them, the dead strapped across the led cavalry horses or in front
of the troopers. Finally the hard pressed men reached the creek, behind which
Gregg reestablished his line, Miles returning to Fussell's Mill to take position
on the right flank of our corps. And Mott had been threatening the enemy
along Bailey's Creek with a strong skirmish line to learn their force, finding
their works strongly held everywhere.

General Birney, "Old Mass and Charge," proposed that we assault at five
o'clock that afternoon, but the force the advance of his skirmish line developed
made him abandon this idea. Besides, about then Gregg's line before Deep Creek
was so strongly attacked as to compel him to cross the creek to the bank nearest
us to sustain himself, it seeming clear enough that an advance would only
bring us disaster. General Grant gave up the idea of pressing the movement
further, determining though, as in July, that we must hold a threatening position
for a few days longer to keep the heavy force of the enemy in our front while he
launched a force from the other flank at the Weldon Road.

The night of the 16th we took position close to the enemy's works and began
to throw up intrenchments. By morning, working in relays, we had a strong
line of works thrown up right under the enemy's nose. Our position, that of the
Eleventh, lay along the side of a steep hill, so that the battery crowning it could
fire directly over our heads. Here we lay the 17th, so near the enemy that we
could see into his works from the crest of the hill. The picket lines, really heavy
skirmish ones, kept up a steady fire all along the line until in the afternoon of
the 17th, when General Grant allowed a flag of truce to be sent out and a truce
arranged to continue from four to six o'clock. Perhaps, springing from this
truce, there was an almost voluntary cessation of firing between the pickets until
a little after five o'clock in the afternoon of the next day, the 18th, when it broke
out with a fury that indicated a pending assault on us.

The skylarking and frolic of the men ceased as the fire of the skirmishers
increased in rapidity and volume, and every man went to his post sober and alert.
Suddenly the battery behind us opened with a roar, our skirmishers came flying
out of the woods and over our works, while behind them sounded the wild yell of
a rebel charging column. As soon as our skirmishers were over our works, the
herculean form of our Sergeant Young bringing up the rear, to be struck by a
bullet as he leaped the parapet. As soon as they were out of the line of fire we
opened a terrible fire, every man loading and firing for his life, but steadily,
swiftly the heavy columns of the enemy poured from the woods, yelling and firing
wildly, those behind pushing those in front, until it seemed as if the pande-
monium of shrieking, rushing demons would roll over our works, by sheer weight
of numbers, in spite of the fire mowing their front lines down. And just then,
as if to complete our destruction, for to lose our line and be driven back into
the tangled woods just at night, chased by a superior foe, far from a supporting
column, meant the loss of our batteries and Andersonville for hundreds of us.

Just then the 100th New York, on our right, broke and left their part of the works in spite of shrieking officers, General Foster himself dashing among them, yelling like a madman and brandishing his sword in a vain attempt to hold them. But the old 10th Connecticut had been held on reserve and was just rushing to the support of the Eleventh, and the men of the two regiments confident of each others support, strung along the gap like lightning until they had filled it after a manner, every man redoubling his efforts to hold the enemy, now surging at the rough abatis planted in the front of our hastily built line.

They had stood our terrible fire well until now, but they could not stand the cold steel we were ready to meet them with should they persist in crossing the works ; they wavered, broke and fell back into the heavy woods between us.

That this was one of the most stubborn assaults of the war is shown by its lasting for twenty minutes, during which time General Walker of the Second Corps notes in his history of that corps, that the fire of musketry was tremendous.

Scarcely had we breathed ourselves, when word was passed that we were to retire at dark, and that we must do so very quietly, without noise or gun rattling, even the tin cups and plates of the men must be so placed in their haversacks as not to give out the monotonous clinking that usually tells that a line of troops is on the march. Then a little latter we stole through the dark woods, leaving Colonel Plaisted with a thousand men of various commands to cover our retreat to a new position. This change of position, or " contraction of the line " as the military historians call it, was rendered necessary to let Mott's divison march away to Petersburgh to take the place of the Ninth Corps in the intrenchments there, so that Corps could support Warren's movement on the Weldon road. Nothing of interest took place in the remainder of the movement, and finally, after a few days spent in skirmishing and reconnoitering in the unrealized hope that a weak spot might be discovered in the enemy's line, we fell back to the river ; the Second Corps and Gregg's cavalry went to Petersburgh, and we returned to our camp at Deep Bottom.

We had been away from it a week, a week of disaster to the regiment, and especially to D, for nineteen of the best men of the company had been killed or wounded during it—one half of its available duty members—and as its thin line filed into the familiar company street those that remained behind gave it a sober greeting, looking sadly for the many familiar faces they would never see again, it is no wonder the eyes of all were dimmed, or that emotional tender-hearted Sergeant Francis should break into tears of manly mourning. We slept the deep sleep of exhaustion in our rude canvas homes that night, but the next night, in the early darkness, the regiment was suddenly ordered to fall in and the men soon found themselves across the ponton bridge and on the road to Bermuda Hundred. Then it was whispered that we were on our way to take part in an assault to be made on the Howlett House Battery at daybreak. It is not strange that we were more surprised than gratified at this proof of confidence in our assaulting abilities, nor is it to be wondered at that the men murmured wrathfully at the idea of assaulting so strong an intrenched position as they knew the Howlett House one to be, armed with heavy guns, and always strongly supported. But for all their hopelessness they would have dashed forward none the less gallantly at the word of command, for they had seen too many dead men lately to fear death greatly, or to hope that if Richmond was to be taken they could long escape him ; in short, had about adopted the philosophy of the old Confederate Colonel, who, in Magruder's desperate charge at Malvern Hill, was heard to shout to his shrinking men, " Forward men, Forward! Do you expect to live forever?" But we were not put to the test, for while we were yet *en route* a galloping aid brought us word that the idea of the assault had been abandoned, and we returned to our camp.

BEFORE PETERSBURGH.

The brigade broke camp at Deep Bottom the 26th of August and marched to a position in the lines before Petersburgh, pitching the camp near the Jerusalem Plank Road. The routine of our duty as closely investing troops ran thus : one day of twenty-four hours we would be on the picket line in our front, placed along a run that intersected an exposed field, the enemy's picket line lying on the other side of the run. Here in the head-high holes some of our predecessors had dug, we shivered through the night, and broiled through the day, not daring to lift our heads above our rude earth-works until dark ; firing and observing through the rude embrasures the banks of earth before our picket-holes were pierced with. When relieved, always at night, and just after dark, we would only fall back into the front line of works, (batteries connected by infantry parapets,) to remain there forty-eight hours. Then relieved by in-coming pickets we would fall back to our camp and remain until morning, the next day being spent on fatigue duty, strengthening the lines of works. Then after another twenty-four hours spent in camp we went on picket again. All this time in camp and out of it, we were under fire, the bullets of the enemy ever singing around our ears, whether we were on the picket line, the main one, the reserve one or in camp, an invested one lying behind a parapet and flanked with batteries of field pieces and gatling guns. And often in camp, in the night, a sudden commotion would take place, to tell that some poor fellow had been severely wounded or perhaps killed, while curling up to his tent-mate under their blankets. But we dreaded the picket line the most, especially the day hours of it, not on account of its danger, for it was a comparatively safe one, all knowing the danger of exposure and conforming to the necessity of keeping closely covered, but to lay for so many hours under a hot sun in a hole in the ground, with only "hard tack" and greasy boiled pork to eat, and the warm water of our—the night before filled—canteens to drink was very disagreeable. Then the certainty that a rush of the enemy meant death or imprisonment for all pickets on the line of attack was not a quieting one.

It was on this picket line that First-Sergeant Bassett was killed the night of the 15th of September. It was a bright, moonlight night, we had just relieved the 1st Maryland, our men crept forward, each squad well informed of its assigned position, and all suddenly hurried for their positions, getting under cover as speedily as possible, the relieved pickets stealing as quietly away for the main line. This was the method of relieving here, but this night some of the relieved pickets moved up the hill somewhat carelessly, their plates and cups clanking noisily and themselves visible in the bright moonlight, so drawing a sharp fire from the enemy's pickets, by which several of the careless fellows were wounded.

Sergeant Bassett was to enter the extreme left picket hole to be occupied by our regiment. Lieutenant Maxfield returned from leave, and commanding D again, was assisting in placing the line, and was in the picket hole when Sergeant Bassett came running to it, in a crouching position, just as the enemy opened fire on the careless Maryland men. Reaching it, Captain Maxfield says, the Sergeant thoughtlessly stood erect on the edge of the pit, while saying, " Well, boys, I'm here," then fell forward into the Lieutenant's arms, a bullet having pierced his throat. Sergeant Bassett was my friend and tent-mate as well as my comrade. Only the night before his death he had talked long of the soon coming end of his term of service, a service he considered already ended by the law of right, he having enlisted on the 7th day of September three years before. But the constituted authorities considered that the three years he had enlisted for must date from October 19th, the date of his muster into service. The point was acknowledged to be a debatable one and Bassett was told that it was his privilege to stay in camp if he chose not to expose himself to the chances of the front line. But Frank was too high spirited a man to split hairs with his honor ; he was either a soldier or a civilian, and if held would be as a soldier and not as a prisoner, declaring that until he was free to go North he would be with D wherever its lot was cast. And with D our bright, brave, true-hearted comrade died, heaping the measure of his duty with his life. The tour of duty in the main line, although affording more liberty of movement, was a dangerous one, especially for those stationed in front of the " Elliott " salient of the Confederates. It was under this salient that the mine had been exploded in the dim of a July morning. From its protruding point hundreds of men had been hurled from sleep into eternity, and for its mutilated possession hundreds more had died. From this grim point of the Confederate line, the hillside before it rough with hillocks of bare earth and rugged with yawning chasms, the result of the explosion, the enemy kept up a sharp and almost continuous night fire, for it was so close to our line that pickets were not thrown out before it by either side. And on dark nights their artillery at this point of the line would be frequently fired to throw a flashing light over the rough ground between the lines of works. Our heavy artillery was not averse to trying its weight with the Confederates at any time. General Humphreys praises the proficiency attending the gunners of this branch of artillery service in silencing the fire of the batteries of the enemy. They had an especial fancy for every now and then opening just at sunrise with every gun they had a roaring, shrieking salute to his rising majesty. Sometimes they did it for practice, sometimes to disconcert and alarm the enemy, sometimes to jubilate over some advantage some one of our armies had somewhere gained. One morning at daybreak, when a detachment of the regiment, including D, was in the little horseshoe shaped outwork we had before " Fort Hell," a messenger came along the line to let us know that at sunrise all our heavy guns would open. I was awake and in charge of a line of guards along the line of D, while the rest of the men, tired with a sleepless night watch, were dozing and napping here and there, crouching, lying, leaning in all possible positions but an erect one, but every man with his rifle clutched by a hand. It was my duty to awaken them and acquaint them with the coming bombardment, but I thought it would be a good joke to let the roar of the guns do the awakening. In a few minutes it came, a sudden roaring of batteries and the shrieking and bursting of shells just as the first ray of sunlight flashed from the east. The men of D not awake, awoke promptly, every man after his nature, some plunging for the bomb-proof, some springing for the parapet, and some just jumping to their feet and whirling around and around during a minute or so of desperate bewilderment. The men who leaped to the parapet to repel any coming enemy thought it a very good joke indeed, the momentarily bewildered ones had seen better jokes, but the ones that plunged for the bomb-proof were loud in expressing their indignation at the severest joke of their experience. It was on this line that the informal election was held by the regiment, Lincoln or McClellan, and the only vote cast for McClellan in D was by stout old Private Maddox. When rallied on his "disloyal" choice, as many preferred patriots thought it, Maddox wrathfully shouted, "My grandfather was a democrat, my father was a democrat, and by the Almighty, I'll not go back on either of them." If his argument did not convince his questioners of the soundness of his logic, his blazing eyes and stalwart form gave it a respectful consideration.

Private Maddox was not a conventional thinker anyway. On Strawberry Plains when a bullet went zipping through his cap, instead of raising a loud thanksgiving for his narrow escape, just by the hair of his head, he boiled over with rage at the injury to his cap, vowing that if he could get his hands on the rebel who fired the damaging shot, he would whip him within an inch of his scoundrelly life.

The twenty-four hours passed in camp gave us time for necessary domestic labors—washing, mending, gun and equipment cleaning. Though still under fire, we were released from the necessity of bearing guns and accoutrements, for which reason these few hours were looked forward to as a sort of turning out to grass, and as gladly as any old horse ever scuttled out of harness to roll in the clover, did we strip off our galling belts to stretch ourselves and enjoy our short space of comparative liberty, those of us not so unfortunate as to lose it in some detail of fatigue or other detested duty. Thus time ran in the entrenchments before Petersburgh until the 24th of September, when we moved back to a distance from the line of fire, making a new camp and giving an opportunity for the commanding officers to gratify their passion for drills, they revelling, according to Captain Maxfield's diary, both the 26th and the 27th in Company and Battalion drills.

THE NORTH SIDE OF THE JAMES.

In the afternoon of the 28th of September we left this camp and marched for Deep Bottom, arriving there in the early morning very tired and sleepy. This was a hard march, so hard a one that when the Second Corps made it on their return from Deep Bottom in August, General Hancock considered it a very exhausting night march for troops to make that were to attack in the morning.

Night marches are particularly weary ones. The monotony of plodding through silent darkness, hour after hour, is as wearing to the men as is the distance.

It is rarely that a gleam of enjoyment illumines the dullness of such a march; but as we plodded along through the darkness of this night and were passing a half slumbering camp, the fires were low and the lights were few, a voice rang out from it calling, "What regiment's that?" At the answer "The Eleventh Maine," a wild yell came from the quiet camp, dark forms rising from it in groups and companies, to shout in stentorian volleys "Who stole the butter?" It was the 98th New York, the regiment that sailed in the old Cahawba with us from Yorktown to Morehead City, on which cruise the sutler of the 98th lost his never to be recovered tubs of butter, and the question now waking the echoes of the dark night was the one to which even a drum-head court-martial failed to find the answer. The expedition we were a part of was intended to surprise the Confederate works on the north side of the river, where they were known to be thinly guarded. It was hoped that our unexpected onslaught would not only force their covering lines, such as the works before Deep Bottom and along Bailey's Creek and the works centering on Fort Harrison, near Chapin's Bluff, but would enable us to get possession of Fort Gilmer, of their main line too, really the key to the position of Chapin's Bluff.

General Ord, now commanding the Eighteenth Corps, was in immediate command of the expedition, consisting of all of the Tenth and Eighteenth Corps that could be spared from the investing lines and of Kautz's cavalry division. Ord was to cross the river from his Bermuda Hundred front, crossing by a ponton bridge laid down at Aiken's in the darkness of the night, we were marching through, was to gain the Varina road, here abutting on the river, move up sharply in the early morning and assail the enemy, taking such works as he could, at all events was to prevent the enemy from crossing troops by the ponton bridge between Drury's and Chapin's Bluffs, to attack Birney's Tenth Corps. Birney's Tenth Corps was to cross the river at Deep Bottom in the early morning, gain the New Market and Darbytown roads—lying beyond the Varina road in the order named and running along the river and parallel with it—the infantry to move along the New Market road with Kautz's cavalry moving on their flank by the Darbytown road, the line to overrun the Confederate outworks before Deep Bottom and sweep forward towards Fort Gilmer's flank, while Ord attacked its front. We moved through Deep Bottom, crushed the light force found before it and moved rapidly up the New Market road, driving the enemy before us. Ord had followed the river road and attacked so strongly with Burnham's brigade as to carry all before him, capturing Fort Harrison with sixteen guns and a large number of prisoners. General Burnham was killed in the assault on the fort. General Ord then moved his forces to the right and left of Fort Harrison, capturing two batteries of three guns each. He then endeavored to sweep down from the captured intrenchments and take the works on the river bank that covered the enemy's ponton bridge, but the Confederate gunboats opening the attempt was unsuccessful.

General Ord was severely wounded in directing this movement, and General Heckman took command of the Eighteenth Corps, but scattered his brigades in the woods so that he could not concentrate them on Fort Gilmer until it had been so heavily reenforced that he was repulsed with a heavy loss. In the meantime, we of the Tenth Corps had captured the enemy's outworks lying across the New Market and Darbytown roads, and were making ready to move on his main line a little over a half mile to their rear. General Grant was now on the ground. Sending our division over to the Darbytown road, about a mile across from the New Market one, to support Kautz, he directed Birney to move forward with his other brigades. Then Ames' division and Brigadier-General William Birney's colored brigade moved on Fort Gilmer by the New Market road, but they were forced back by the grape and musketry when so close to the works that some of the colored brigade jumped into the ditch and tried to climb to the parapet of the fort by each other's shoulders. We of Terry's Division were now pushing through the captured works, Kautz on the right, all moving under a heavy fire and in momentary expectation that the assault on Gilmer would be successful, when we proposed to force our way into Richmond. So vigorously did we move forward that when the announcement of the failure of the assault reached us we were actually less than four miles from Richmond, and it required rapid movement and severe fighting on our part to get out of the precarious position our own sanguine advance had placed our inadequate force in. Rejoining our line, light works were thrown up in the night.

The next day was one of heavy skirmishing only, until the afternoon, when a heavy force of the enemy assaulted Fort Harrison and were beaten back three times before abandoning their attempt to recapture it. General Stannard who so gallantly held the fort for us, lost his arm in the second assault. While these north side operations where going on, General Meade was moving on the left, partly to keep reenforcements from the north side, where so much was hoped for, and partly to try to gain ground on that flank. The results of his movements were desultory, although rather in his favor. We held our now well intrenched position on the north side of the James with only heavy skirmishing, while threatening demonstrations were made by brigades of both sides from day to day, but without a real collision until the 7th of October. The right flank of our force on that side of the river—our brigade held the extreme infantry position on that flank—was covered by Kautz's cavalry. His position was across a swamp from us, on the Darbytown road at the Confederate line of intrenchments we captured the 29th of September. Here he had 1700 men and two batteries. So threatening was this position that two divisions of Confederates moved out the night of October 6th, and at sunrise of the 7th attacked on his front and his right flank. He could not stand up against such an attack as this, and in falling back through the swamp, by the narrow road crossing it, found the rebel cavalry there before him. Leaving them his eight guns, his men made desperate attemps to get under the wing of our division, scouting through the woods in flying groups. About as soon as the roar of the enemy's sudden attack on Kautz came to our ears the advance of his broken cavalry squadrons came dashing through the woods on our flank, riding recklessly through tearing brambles and matted copses. Almost immediately our division left its intrenchments at the double-quick for a position at about right angles to the one left, quickly forming front to intercept the enemy's advancing force, now closely following Kautz's flying men. But as the enemy swept through the woods he fell on the heavy skirmish line we had thrown out, and his immediate advance was halted until assaulting columns could be formed. At last his heavy columns were ready for the assault and his skirmishers began to press ours in an attempt to break them, their columns hoping to get close to our line under cover of an advancing skirmish line.

But our men were stubborn. I remember that Colonel Plaisted sent me with orders to Lieutenant Dunbar, in command of the skirmishers of our regiment. The fire was furious, and the lines lay close on each other, it was a murderous one, but neither Dunbar nor his men were inclined to yield an inch. "We can hold a line of battle" yelled one bold Yankee. But they couldn't, for when the roar of the assault came rolling through the dense woods in which the fight took place, we had to hold the fire of our line until the flying skirmishers should get behind us, in this way getting the shrieking, dingy lines of the enemy within short rifle range before we opened on them. The grey lines pressed forward through the hail storm of bullets our brigade was pouring on them, when suddenly from our left broke out the volley roar of the seven-shooters of the New Hampshire men. Seven volleys in one. Flesh and blood could not stand such a cyclone of lead ; and they stopped, broke and fled, leaving the woods piled with their dead and dying. Just as our victory was assured, reenforcements came up the road on the double-quick, to protect our extreme right. Panting and exhausted as they were with their efforts to reach us in time to be of service, they had breath enough left to give hearty cheers for our stand-up victory. We are particularly proud of this victory, as we won it without the protecting works so necessary to break the headlong impetus of an assaulting force, and in beating off the enemy's heavy charging columns stood in about single rank, having to stretch our line to a length that would oppose any flanking movement the enemy might combine with his front attack. And curiously enough our right regiment, the 10th Connecticut, just lapped the enemy's lines. I can see the 10th now as it stood on our immediate right, every man of it fighting with impetuous vigor to protect our flank, even its Chaplain, Henry Clay Trumbull, vying with the rest of its officers in encouraging their men, not only by his words but by flourshing a most unclerical looking revolver. It was here that Chaplain Trumbull won the name of " Fighting Chaplain " and high honors as he has since won in his chosen calling as Editor of the *Sunday School Times*, I'll venture that he is prouder of the title he received from the rank and file on that day of mortal warfare than of any theological one his service in the spiritual army has brought him. In this affair of the New Market Road, of D, its Commander, Lieutenant Maxfield and Corporal Horace Whittier of the Color Guard, were wounded.

The 13th of October our regiment was part of a force that moved out on the Darbytown road on a reconnoissance in force. We found the enemy's works of the most formidable character and strongly held. A brigade of Ames' division assaulted a promising part of them, but was beaten back, and a movement of ours made in conjunction with that of Ames, failed, we falling back under a very heavy artillery and musketry fire. While we lay in the woods before these inhospitable works, this storm of war sweeping over us, the cooks of D, then

John Day and Prince Dunifer, appeared with camp kettles filled with hot coffee, and persisted in serving it to the men in spite of the great danger they had to expose themselves to in doing so. Cook Day, always excited in action, was none the less so that he was running the risk he then was, and as some slow member of the company lying flat upon the ground would fumble for his tin cup as John stood over him, John's ire would boil till he would shout in that stentorian voice of his, "Hurry up, hurry; do you want me to be killed?" And so amusing was John's tribulations to Prince Dunifer, walking behind John to carry the reserve kettle, that he forgot all about his own danger in laughing at John. But neither John nor Prince ever shirked a duty or a danger—both good cooks and good fighters, John only excelling in the intensity with which he performed every duty, whether it was to cook, fight or to run away. Who is more worthy of honor than are these comrades? They followed our marching column day after day, loaded with kettles, spades and provisions, at every opportunity making hot coffee and taking it to the men on the line of skirmish or battle ; at night preparing a fiery bean hole in which to bake their beans, standing guard all night if need be over the simmering delicacies, that in the morning their men might have something tangible for their belts to tighten over. And what welcome did a rushing reenforcement meet with at some desperate moment of a raging battle, equal to the one that used to greet old John Day as he came plunging through the woods to our hungry, shivering line on some gray morning, his broad shoulders sturdily bearing a yoke from which depended kettles of steaming coffee and smoking beans. Of D, Private Woodbury was the only man wounded on this expedition.

In the latter part of October, Grant pushed a strong force from the left towards the South Side Railroad. In connection with the movement we made one on the right.

Moving out at daylight of the 27th of October, we drove the enemy's pickets in on the Darbytown and the Charles City roads, and moved forward to threaten their works without intending to assault them. While we were maneuvering before the works, General Weitzel, in command of the Eighteenth Corps, was moving with that corps to turn the Confederate left flank by pushing through White Oak Swamp and taking possession of the unoccupied rebel works on the Williamsburgh and New Bridge roads ; then was to move on Richmond. But General Longstreet, now in command of the Confederate forces on the north side of the James, anticipated the movements so effectually that Weitzel found the supposed-to-be unoccupied works so thoroughly occupied as to make his attack on them a complete failure, he losing heavily in both men and colors, each of his two attacking brigades losing three colors. About the hour of the afternoon that Weitzel met with this defeat, we were ordered to press our demonstrations and, if possible, to carry the works. The attempts made to carry out this order were unsuccessful. We had to lie on the ground in the rain that night to cover the retreat of Weitzel's men, who wearily plodded back through the rain, mud and darkness, not reaching a safe position in our rear until early morning. We then moved back into our own works. On the 29th of October our cavalry pickets were driven in from their position of observation on Johnson's farm, the position that Kautz was driven from on the 7th of the month. Anticipating an attack of the same sort as was the one we then repelled, our division moved out across the intervening swamp Kautz left his guns in. Reaching a position on the other side, we formed a strong skirmish line and charged the captured picket works, the enemy running from them as we neared them. Sergeant Brady of D was wounded as we entered the now recaptured works. This was the last engagement of the war on the north side of the James.

CHAPIN'S FARM.

The night of the 7th of October we bivouaced on the ground of Chapin's farm that we had fought for during the day, not thinking that we should remain in nearly the same position until the Spring campaign opened. But we did, first pitching our camp near the bivouac ground to move out from on expeditions into the enemy's country, finally building our winter quarters on the camp ground. But before the regiment went into winter quarters the three years service its original members yet remaining with the regiment had entered upon had ended, and the preparations for the mustering out of those of them who had not reenlisted were completed. And on the 2d day of November, after taking leave of their old comrades, these freed veterans marched away from the colors they had helped place in the front of many battles. Jubilant as they undoubtedly were, happy in anticipation of the coming meeting with loved ones, there was yet a visible tinge of sadness in their parting from the old comrades to remain and endure the hardships and privations they themselves would no more know. And those left behind with the colors, though they sped their parting comrades with hearty good will, could not help a faint heart sinking at the thought that perhaps before they could march away to their homes the fate of hundreds they had known might be theirs, and they too be lying in the shallow graves hurrying burying parties can only spare the time to give the dead of a battle field But there was little time given the men remaining with the colors for sentimental considerations. The day after their comrades left for Maine, they in company with the 10th Connecticut, marched to Deep Bottom and sailed from there to Fortress Monroe, where a provisional division was forming to proceed to New York City for the purpose of keeping the peace there during the pending Presidential election. This division, consisting of the 11th Maine, the 6th, 7th and 10th Connecticut regiments, the 3d and 7th New Hampshire, the 13th Indiana, 112th New York, Battery M, of the 1st U. S. Artillery and other troops, was under the command of General Hawley, and sailed from Fortress Monroe the 4th of November, the Eleventh being one of the regiments on the steamer General Lyon.

Lieutenant Maxfield was in command of the Eleventh at this time, as he, a reenlisted veteran, was the ranking officer with the regiment, so many of its officers had been mustered out by the reason of the expiration of their terms of service, or were detached on headquarters service. Arriving in New York harbor the morning of the 6th of November, on the morning of the 7th the troops landed at Fort Richmond, on Staten Island, and went on board steamers which took them to points along the river front of New York City. The 11th Maine, 3d New Hampshire, 13th Indiana and 112th New York regiments and Battery M, of the 1st U. S. Artilery, went on board the ferryboat Westfield and proceeded to Pier 42, North River. The force lay there through the 8th (election day), the 9th and 10th, and until the 11th, when the authorities becoming satisfied that the knowledge of the short, sharp fate rioting mobs would meet with at the hands of the grim veterans on the river front, had secured a peaceful election period; the force returned to Fort Richmond, and after a couple of days spent in this stronghold, embarked the 14th (the Eleventh on the steamer North Point), and put to sea that night. Arriving at Fortress Monroe, the provisional division formation was discontinued and the regiments proceeded each to its own camp ground, the Eleventh reaching its camp ground on Chapin's Farm the 17th of November. In its camp, in charge of the guard left to care for the regimental baggage, the regiment found 201 recruits to be distributed through its skeleton companies. The strengthened Eleventh then proceeded to prepare its winter quarters. The personnel and the organization of the regiment of the winter of 1865 were largely changed from what they were when the regiment first landed at Bermuda Hundred. For the field and staff, it was now Colonel Hill instead of Colonel Plaisted, Lieutenant-Colonel Baldwin instead of Lieutenant-Colonel Spofford, Adjutant Fox had accepted a commission in a regiment destined for adventurous service among the Indians of the western frontier, and Chaplain Wells had gone to sow his pearls of truth in a less porcine parish, and its companies were about as completely changed. Take D for a fair example—Captain Mudgett was still a prisoner ; First Lieutenant Sellmer, who had been on detached service at division headquarters for months, was promoted to the Captaincy of Company B ; Second Lieutenant Maxfield, who had been made First Lieutenant of D when Lieutenant Sellmer was promoted, was now made Captain of H, a rapid promotion but fairly won by his conspicuous service in the campaign just ended, where he had shown marked executive ability as commanding officer of D since the 2d of June, when he took up the charge Captain Mudgett then laid down. Lieutenant Perkins, who joined the company in July as Second Lieutenant, had been promoted to First Lieutenant and was now the commanding officer of D. Of the Sergeants of D in May, Bassett was dead, Blake was yet a prisoner, Francis had been mustered out, Brady was First Lieutenant of Company I, and the only one remaining with the company was Young, now its Second Lieutenant, a deserved honor for the gallantry he had displayed in many engagements, and for the fidelity with which he had served the company as Acting First Sergeant in 1862, and again in 1863, and as Acting First Sergeant and First Sergeant in 1864. Of the Corporals and Privates making up the strength of D when it landed at Bermuda Hundred, some had been killed, many had died of wounds, many more were too disabled by wounds to reenter active service, and others had served their full three years and had been mustered out. Although the Eleventh Maine of the campaign of 1865 was largely different in material and organization from that of 1864, yet the work it did in the assault on Petersburgh and in the pursuit of Lee showed that the regiment was still worthy of its honored name. The changes were not confined to the regiment. A new brigade commander was given us in Colonel Dandy of the 100th New York, the ranking Colonel of the brigade now that Colonel Plaisted had resigned, General Foster had become division commander, and the corps

56

was no longer the Tenth, but the Twenty-fourth, and in command of General Gibbon, formerly a division commander of the Second Corps, while the army of the James was now commanded by General Ord, formerly of the Eighteenth Corps, which corps was now the Twenty-fifth. The newly organized Twenty-fourth Army Corps was fortunate in its composition of veteran troops, and in its commander a West Pointer with a practical military experience since the opening of the war and always in positions of responsibility, till his bravery and his devotion to every duty devolving on him had won him the command of the corps. Though a strict disciplinarian, and a stern man at need, as we soon found, General Gibbon was a kindly man and with a bit of sentiment in his make-up, for when he selected a heart as a badge for our new corps he promulgated an order in which he said : "The symbol selected testifies our affectionate regard for all our brave comrades, alike the living and the dead, and our devotion to our sacred cause." True and well said, every word touching a sympathetic chord, and for this assurance that he was one with them in sympathy, hope and devotion, the hearts of his men went out to the General, and from then on he could look for unswerving fidelity from both officers and men. A happy begining for the new corps ; contributing no little to the brilliancy of its services in the short and glorious campaign of 1865, when it assaulted and carried strongly entrenched and strongly held positions, and marched day and night with a speed and endurance unequalled in the history of the war, until it flung itself across Lee's path and withstood the last charge of the Army of Northern Virginia.

The winter of 1864-5 was passed by our men in the rude huts they erected of logs, boards and canvas, getting height by digging a few feet into the ground, sealing and flooring the sunken portion. These huts were heated by sheet iron stoves, and were fitted up with ingeniously contrived bunks and home-made furniture, so that the men were very comfortable in them ; the officers were really no more so in their more commodious log houses with their chimneys fitted with fire places. The duties of the winter were the usual military ones of drill, fatigue, guard, and picket, supplemented by the carrying out of an order to have the troops in line of battle every morning at from shortly before daybreak until sunrise, that they might rush to the parapets and repel any attempted surprise by the enemy, who were doubtless standing in a shivering line behind their works as we were behind ours, both lines with an identical fear. The picket duty, always an uncomfortable one, was particularly so this winter from the extreme cold—a remarkable thing for a Virginia winter—but by keeping great log fires blazing on the reserve lines, and changing the outposts every hour, there was little suffering, no more than the men were willing to endure in consideration of the generous ration of whiskey served out to the relieved pickets as soon as they reached their camps. Winter passed and spring came, and with it the inspections and reviews that indicate impending movement to experienced troops. Finally our corps was reviewed by President Lincoln. It was the first and the last sight we had of our beloved President. And for his sake we will ever have a kind remembrance of the great field of dull green, with enveloping woods, that the review was held in, and of the long steel-tipped lines of troops, and of the gaily appareled cloud of officers galloping behind the plainly dressed man, with the rugged, seamed, but kindly face, whose long legs reached nearly to the ground from the rather short legged horse he was astride of, Mrs. Lincoln rolling along in a carriage behind the reviewing party.

THE FALL OF PETERSBURGH.

General Humphreys says that late in the winter of 1865, General Grant became aware that General Lee had determined to abandon Petersburgh and Richmond in the early spring and unite with General Johnston, then in front of General Sherman, in North Carolina. Briefly the Confederate plan was to evade Grant, crush Sherman, and then face Grant with a united and victorious army. But Grant thought it wise to take the initiative, drive Lee from his intrenchments before he was ready to leave them, and try to crush him before he could unite with Johnston. In response to an invitation from General Grant, General Sherman visited him at City Point, the 27th day of March, and they arranged that Sherman should suddenly move away from his works before Johnston, march northward, and either join Grant before Richmond, or if Lee was moving south— either of his own volition or because driven south—should head him off, and unite with Grant in decimating his forces before he could get aid from Johnston.

That very night, General Ord, in command of the Army of the James, moved from the north side of the James with two divisions of the Twenty-fourth Corps, one of the Twenty-fifth and his cavalry, making a forced march over terrible roads, in the dark, rainy night, and the stormy day succeeding it, we took position at a late hour of the 28th of March in the rear of the Second Corps at Hatcher's Run, having traveled thirty-six miles to do so. The morning of the 28th, General Sheridan had moved out with the cavalry of the Army of the Potomac, and working to the left of our army, sought to reach the right and rear of that of the enemy. This movement was supported on the 29th by the Second and Fifth Corps, when we moved to the front to take the position vacated by the Second Corps. This movement to the left had the effect desired by General Grant, General Lee strongly reenforcing the force opposing Sheridan, having to weaken his lines before Petersburgh to do so. Sheridan pressed forward the 29th, the 30th, the 31st, the enemy growing in his front as he forced them backwards until April 1st, when with his cavalry force and the Fifth Corps he fought the battle of Five Forks, capturing Pickett, 4,500 men, 13 colors and 6 guns.

While the battle of Five Forks was raging, General Grant, from information brought him from Sheridan, pushed the Second Corps forward to carry the enemy's intrenchments, those to our left. Their attack failed. The order issued by Grant that night called for an sssault in the early morning of the 2d of April, by the Sixth, the Ninth and so much of our corps as Ord had marched across the river. The Sixth Corps, on our immediate right (the Ninth Corps lying beyond it) was to break the enemy's line. Its formidable attack, calculated to carry any sort of work it might find before it, and howsoever defended, was made at daylight by its three divisions, formed by brigades with regimental front, and swept all before it, quickly beating down the enemy's sharp resistance and capturing a long line of three miles with many guns and prisoners. The Ninth

Corps attacked at the same time, taking the works so familiar to us, on both sides of the Jerusalem Plank Road, but finding a line of works in the rear of those they captured, and strongly held by General Gordon's Corps, they made no further advance. The Eleventh had moved out to the front the 29th of March with the rest of its corps, when the Second Corps moved to the left. The night of the 29th the regiment lay in the woods before an outlying line of the enemy. The 30th it pressed forward with its division, driving the enemy into their works. The picket line of the regiment then thrown out before the part of their works in our front, becoming heavily engaged, company after company was sent to its reenforcement until the whole regiment was engaged. In its immediate front, just across a wide slashing, and sweeping our lines, was a rebel battery. Its fire became so distressing to our men, that they determined to silence it. Carefully concentrating their fire upon its guns mounted *en barbette*, it was not long before the battery's fire slackened, and was finally completely silenced, the gunners flatly refusing to man their guns in the face of the uninterrupted storm of bullets sweeping across the parapet. Night came on with the regiment in the same position it had occupied during the day. As it grew dark we fell back into the woods a few rods. Then a numerous fatigue party, made up from the regiments of the brigade, was sent out to throw up a line of intrenchments, a heavy picket line covering this fatigue work, with the regiments of the brigade some rods in the rear lying in line of battle behind their stacked guns. Towards morning the monotonous roll of picket firing that had been kept up during the night suddenly rose in volume on our immediate front, then the charging yell of a rebel line of battle brought every man of us to his feet. Well, within a minute the brands of the low burning bivouac fires were scattered to the right and left, that their flickering light might not serve the enemy to pour a volley into us by, (I can see Sergeant Keene jumping and kicking with characteristic promptness and vigor at the brands of a fire I) had,) and we had seized our guns, set up an answering yell, and were rushing through the darkness at the oncoming enemy. At our yell the enemy, who had run over our pickets, expecting to surprise us, supposing our line of battle to be lying right behind the picket one, the momentum of their charge gone, their blow delivered in the air, our yell rising from an unexpected position, caused them to stand, irresolute and uncertain, for the brief moment we needed in which to reach the just thrown up works, works that the enemy was not aware of the existence of, and that the darkness prevented their seeing, and occupying the reverse side of as a cover against our counter charge, they halting within a rod or so of them. And before they could realize their exposed position, and in spite of the loudly expressed determination of our Brigade Commander, that they should not, the men of the Eleventh had opened so severe a fire on the dark mass of agitated figures that could be dimly seen against a background of lightening sky, that those of the enemy who did not throw themselves flat upon the ground to escape it, and remain so until daylight when they gave themselves up as prisoners, went fleeing through the darkness pursued by a storm of bullets, losing heavily in the progress of their escape. General Dandy did not remonstrate against the orders the officers of the Eleventh were giving their men to fire, out of regard for the Confederates, but in the confusion and darkness of the hour he had lost the position of his regiments, and was really confident that the mass of men in our front was composed of our own troops. To solve the question it was shouted to those men "What regiment is that?" "The Eleventh," was the answer, "The Eleventh what?" They would not answer the question. Could it be that it was really a part of our regiment in advance of us? We could not clearly see the length of a company, much less that of our regiment, so could not make sure by observing the length of our line that we were not behind a part of our own regiment. "Who's your Colonel?" cried a voice to them, "Colonel Davis," was the answer, and "Fire, Fire," rang out along our line, and the rolling volleys did their dreadful work. It was the Eleventh Mississippi that stood before us, and Colonel Davis, their Colonel was in command of the assaulting brigade. This was the morning of April 1st. We lay behind the new but already christened works that day, with a heavy and constantly engaged skirmish line before us. At night we went into position for the assault of the morning of the 2d, spending the night largely in listening to the tremendous roar of the cannon bombarding the Confederate lines, waiting in suspense until we should move forward at the signal—a cannon shot from a particular point—that should send the Sixth Corps men through the stubborn works before us. It was so dark a night that it was nearly 5 o'clock before the troops could see to move at all intelligently, and then they could see but a few yards before them. But at the cannon shot the massed brigades of the Sixth moved forward rapidly, broke the enemy's picket line, and poured over their main defenses. At this moment our own picket line, a heavy one, and reenforced by the brigade sharp shooters, picked men, commanded by Lieutenant Payne, all under command of Captain Maxfield, as brigade officer of the day, who the Captain had pressed forward during the night until they were close under the works in our front, at this movement they were ordered to charge, and regardless of the opposing numbers, dashed over the abatis and into the Confederate works, laying about them so vigorously that the enemy viewed them as part of an advancing line of battle, throwing down their rifles and surrendering in such numbers that Captain Maxfield seemed to be in command of a small section of the rebel army to the brigade as it moved over the works to his support. He had a most efficient coadjutor in caring for his prisoners, and separating them so far from their thrown down rifles as to remove any temptation they might have to pick them up again when they should realize how small a force they had surrendered to, for he had promptly appointed Sergeant Locke, of Company K, as his Provost. "Fall in here, the tallest on the right," shouted that active officer, "Now count off by twos," then it was "Right face, Forward March," and the unarmed Mississippians were swinging off with a firm, military stride, under a new commander.

Promptly making connection with the Sixth Corps advance, General Gibbon moved as with them towards Petersburgh. By arrangement our corps took precedence of the Sixth after crossing the captured works, the Sixth forming on the right and left as a support. Our advance soon reached the Confederate works, advanced before their main inner line, here running up from the Appomattox and along Indian Town Creek. The advanced works we moved directly on were Forts Gregg and Whitworth. Our division was moved to the front and an assault made on these forts.

These forts, especially Gregg, made a desperate defense. General Gibbon says that the assault on this fort was " the most desperate one of the war." It was only taken by a determined bayonet dash led by Lieutenant Payne, of our regiment, who was the first man to leap into the fort and who owed his life to his skill with the use of the saber, a skill acquired as a trooper in Mexico, and in many desperate Indian fights during a term of service on the plains of the west. As Gregg fell, Whitworth was carried, and the first in it too were of the Eleventh, Companies A and B, that had been detached as skirmishers when the regiment crossed the Confederate works in the morning. These companies had driven the enemy's skirmishers through the fields between the enemey's lines of works, finally forcing them into a great area of log barracks flanking Whitworth, when the Confederates made it warm for our men in every way, they setting fire to the barracks, and fighting from street to street of the blazing structures. Finally the rebel skirmishers fell back into Whitworth, A and B then crowded closely to this work, returning its heavy fire with interest, until Turner's brigade of West Virginians moved forward to assault the fort, when the boys of these companies of the Eleventh darted forward at the head of the assaulting column, entering the fort by its sallyport, and the rebels were already throwing down their guns when Turner's men appeared on the scene. Nor were A and B yet satisfied. Anticipating an immediate assault on the enemy's inner and only remaining line of works, these companies pushed across the intervening fields and secured a skirmishing position on Indian Town Creek, where they remained for some time, anxiously looking for an advancing Union column, and fully determined to head it, and if possible be the first armed Yankees to enter the Cockade City. But General Humphreys says the Sixth Corps men were exhausted, having been under arms for eighteen hours now, and it was concluded not to attack further until the next morning. Up to the night of the 2d of April, of D, Privates Tehan, Mathews, Morrill, Ryan, Stratton and Watson were wounded, Privates Ryan and Watson mortally, and Sergeant Gowell, Privates Bickmore, Brien, Findel, Geary, Gibbs, Seavey, Simmonds and Stevens were taken prisoners. Of the prisoners Private Bickmore was wounded when captured. The prisoners from D were taken while on the picket line, when the Mississippians ran over it the morning of April 1st, and Private Peter Haegan would have been added to their list but for his shrewdly begging permission of his captor to be allowed to get the haversack Peter had left at the foot of a tree near the post he was surprised on. The good natured Mississippian allowed him to go the few feet only separating him and his provender bag, but Peter failed to return, preferring to throw himself upon the ground and crawl to the rear until he had reached our line.

THE PURSUIT AND THE SURRENDER.

The morning of the 3d of April it was quickly known that Lee's army had escaped in the direction of Amelia Court House, and that his troops from both Richmond and Petersburgh were concentrating there. But his objective point was the question. Was he intending to move directly west towards Lynchburgh, or southwest for Danville? In either case he must do so through Burkeville Junction, where the Southside and the Richmond and Danville railroads cross each other. Sheridan with his cavalry and the Fifth Corps, followed by Meade with the Second and Sixth Corps, pushed along the south side of the Appomattox River to keep in constant touch of Lee's movements and to strike the Danville road between its crossing the Appomattox at High Bridge and Burkeville Junction, while Ord with the troops of the Twenty-fourth Corps as a flying column, in the lightest possible marching order, should directly push for the Junction, moving along the Southside road, with the Ninth Corps following. We reached the Junction in the night of the 5th, having marched fifty-two miles since the morning of the 3d. And that night General Read, of General Ord's staff, moved towards High Bridge with a small force, his orders requiring him to seize and burn that bridge and those at Farmville, if possible. This by order of General Grant, and transmitted through Sheridan, then at about half-way between Burkeville Junction and Amelia Court House. The morning of the 6th, Ord was notified by Sheridan that Lee was apparently moving on the Junction. As soon as Grant was informed of this, he directed Ord to move to Rice Station, two-thirds of the way towards Farmville, when there we were directly in Lee's road were he pushing for either Lynchburg or Danville. At the same time messengers were hurried to overtake General Read before he should reach High Bridge, where the van of Lee's army already was, but it was too late to save the fated young officer from death, and his small command from almost annihilation. At Rice Station we found Longstreet's Command intrenched and ready for us, Longstreet quite willing to fight for the time Anderson, Ewell and Gordon needed to march by his rear with the wagon trains they were convoying from Amelia Court House. But as it was about night, we contented ourselves with taking position to attack from in the early morning. During this day, the 6th, Sheridan and Meade were constantly attacking Lee's army at every possible point, and successfully, too, for they captured Ewell and his entire command, together with one-half of Anderson's, a large part of Gordon's, and destroyed the greater part of the trains they were making such useless sacrifices for. Longstreet escaped us while we were sleeping before his intrenchments at Rice Station. Marching to Farmville he crossed to the north bank of the Appomattox, and in the morning, that of the 7th, began to move towards Lynchburgh by the road leading through Appomattox Court House. He was followed by Gordon, and he by Mahone. Finding that Longstreet had stolen away, Ord moved on towards Farmville in pursuit, marching by the short cut wagon road Longstreet had gone over, instead of following the railroad to High Bridge. Wright was now following us with the Sixth Corps. All the bridges but one across the Appomattox had been destroyed by the rebels after crossing, and they were in the act of destroying that one, a wagon road bridge near High Bridge, when the Second Corps advance, under Barlow, reached it and saved it.

The Second Corps immediately crossed the Appomattox by this bridge, treading so closely on the heels of the Confederates that General Barlow overtook Gordon's Corps, attacked it and cut off a large part of the wagon train it was covering. So threatening was the Second Corps in its movements, that Lee was forced to halt his force and take a strong position on the crest of a long slope of ground that covered the stage and plank roads leading to Lynchburg. Here he threw up light intrenchments and put artillery in position. After riding along the ground taken up by Lee, General Meade ordered the Second Corps to attack, at the same time sending messengers to Ord to have our division and the Sixth Corps cross the river at Farmville, and help force Lee into a general engagement. But as there was no bridge remaining near us for us to cross by, nor could a fordable place be found, this order could not be obeyed. The Second Corps attack then, unsupported, was but a partial success, but enables General Humphreys, then in command of that Corps, to claim with reason that by the enforced detention due to the vigor and aggressiveness of the movement of the Second Corps, Lee lost the supplies awaiting him at Appomattox Station and gave time for Sheridan with his cavalry and Ord with the Fifth and Twenty-fourth Corps to put themselves across his path at Appomattox Court House. The Second and Sixth Corps pushed directly after Lee the morning of the 8th. He had moved in the night toward Lynchburg. These Corps kept up this direct pursuit until midnight, only halting after making a march of twenty-six miles. The morning of the 8th, the Twenty-fourth and the Fifth Corps pushed out from near Farmville, and accompanied by General Grant and staff, pushed towards Appomattox Court House by the shortest roads. All day long these Corps pressed forward, the men, although tired and footsore, requiring neither urging nor command to put forth every effort to head Lee off from Lynchburg, for all understood that it was Grant's purpose for us to march by Lee's army and head him off, while the Second and Sixth Corps should dog his heels and hamper his speed by forcing him to turn and defend himself at every opportunity they could get. It was a question of legs and endurance now. On and on our men plodded, none falling out until worn out. All were too tired even to raise a cheer in passing General Grant as he was sitting on a roadside log resting himself while enjoying a quiet smoke. And General Ord secured this tribute when, in response to the cries of "Coffee" that ran along the marching line he was riding by to reach the head of the column, he halted it as soon as he gained its advance, that the tired, hungry men might rest a bit while they cooked their coffee, every man his own, in his tin dipper set on one of the hastily lighted roadside fires. Ord was one of the general officers that knew the needs of men. "Get out of the road men," shouted one of his staff as they rode along through a line of men resting in the dusty road. "Stop Sir," said the gray old general sternly, "the men are tired, rein to the roadside and follow that." As the day passed we found ourselves on the track of Sheridan; prisoners, guns and trains of wagons captured by his vigorous advance, lined the roadside, encouraging our tired men to put forth every exertion. Darkness found us still pressing on and it was not until about daybreak that we halted for more than a few minutes rest at a time, the Fifth Corps plodding on at our heels in dogged determination to be there too. At about daylight we reached the vicinity of Appomattox Station, which Sheridan's Cavalry had reached a few hours before, and in time to capture a train of artillery and three trains of cars loaded with subsistence supplies for

Lee's army. Our division halted near the captured cars, and details of our men set to work to divide the fat sides of Virginia bacon they were mainly loaded with, among their regiments, and tired, sleepy, but more hungry than either, we made coffee, greedily ate great slices of uncooked bacon with the few crackers of hard bread yet remaining in the haversacks, thinking it as appetizing and satisfying a meal as we had ever eaten. But we had not fairly wiped the bacon grease from our smacking lips when the roar of guns and the roll of musketry rose from the immediate front, telling us that our cavalry was heavily engaged. Falling in quickly at the sharp voiced orders transmitted from Gibbon down, the men were double quicked on the sound of battle. We soon came up with the retiring cavalry, Crook's and Custer's men stubbornly fighting Gordon's advancing infantry column. As we sped by them into the woods Gordon's men were pushing through, a voice shouted, "There's the Eleventh Maine," and a wild cheer rose from a body of cavalry on our right. It was the First Maryland, now mounted and serving in its own arm of the service. Inspired by this recognition and complimentary tribute, the Eleventh dashed vigorously forward and crossed the road Lee's army was now making its last advance on. The gray lines of Gordon's men were dashing forward as the cavalry fell back behind us, but as the swiftly deploying lines of battle of our division unrolled before them, and the long line of blue-clad men pressed forward to receive them, the last advance of the Army of Northern Virginia became a hasty retreat. Negotiations that had been going on between Grant and Lee by letter for two days were now resumed with the result that we all know of. But while the leaders were conferring, we of the opposing rank and file were not sitting down in the amity the histories of the war indicate we were. Blood was shed on the hills of Appomattox that day. As the column of Gordon fell back in the haste of consternation at the unexpected appearance of infantry in their path, we followed after it, and entering the wide field beyond which the Confederates were drawn up behind planted artillery, we were ordered by General Foster to press across it. Then, though unsupported, the Eleventh pushed forward, and finding its progress contested by the fire of a battery before it, broke into a yell and charged the guns. The swift advance was met not only by a sweep of grape and canister, but by the volley fire of a supporting line of battle. In the confusion the two right companies were separated from the left one, rejoining the regiment as it lay in a protecting declension of the open field before the battery it had sought to capture, grape, canister and bullets sweeping over it in appalling volume. Many of those remaining at the log houses the right companies of the regiment had occupied before rejoining the regiment were captured, the Confederate cavalry pushing forward and enveloping this advance position about the time the main body of the occupying companies abandoned it to rejoin the regiment. To make a short story of it, a number of the Eleventh were killed and wounded before the regiment got out of its untenable position before the battery, which it did by moving down one protecting ravine and up another that led nearly back to the position in the woods it had charged from. It was at the moment of retreat that private Moses E. Sherman, of D, was killed, struck dead at the feet of the First Sergeant of the company, Sergeant Keene, who would not believe his friend dead at first, nor would he leave the field until he was convinced that " Mustache " was dead. Poor little " Mustache!" ever cheerfully smiling, ever ready for lark or duty, more than liked by all of us, it seems hard indeed that one so able and willing to enjoy life, and to make life enjoyable for others, should lie dead on the last battlefield of the war. The lot of the Sherman boys was a hard one. Both original members of the company, both taken prisoners at Fair Oaks to endure the privations of Libby Prison together, both reenlisted, William to be mortally wounded at Deep Bottom in August, '64, and Moses to die in the last charge that our old company was called upon to participate in. Scarcely had the regiment reached a sheltered position, when companies A and B were thrown out as part of a skirmish line forming to cover an attack General Ord was preparing, and this skirmish line was moving swiftly across the field intervening between the battle lines when a galloping aid overtook it and announced Lee's surrender. Besides Private Sherman killed, Private Burns and Curtis of D were wounded in making the assault on the battery, which proved to be a liberal section of the celebrated Washington artillery. The formal surrender of the regiments of the Army of Northern Virginia was made to the Fifth and Twenty-fourth Corps, as they were the Corps that, out marching the Confederates, had closed the road of their retreat. We encamped on the battlefield during the progress of the surrender, and it was not until the men of the last regiment of Lee's Army had stacked arms, laid its ragged colors on the now useless bayonets, and marched mournfully away to ruined homes to begin the world over again, that we took up our line of march for Richmond, the last of the Corps of the Army of the Potomac preceding us by a few days.

AFTER THE SURRENDER.

Our Corps moved towards Richmond in a leisurely and gala-day manner, the bands playing whenever we moved through a village or country "city," (the white flag flying from every house in token of acquiescence in the terms of the surrender.) Our columns, objects of intense curiosity to sway crowds of women and children, white and black, with swarthy, gray clothed veterans peeping grimly from out of the background at the men they had never before been so near except in armed violence. We arrived at Manchester, opposite Richmond, the 25th of April, where we camped for the night. The 26th we entered the city and were received by the occupying troops, troops of the Army of the James, the city having surrendered to General Weitzel's advance from the north side, on the morning of April 3d. There was a marked contrast in the appearance of ourselves and the receiving comrades. They as spick and span as if just turned out of military band boxes, we ragged and dust laden, but as we marched along between their drawn up lines, it was plainly expressed to us that they would gladly be able to change places with Foster's division to bear its prestige of endurance and intrepidity. Nor did the crowds of people thronging the streets we marched through, sidewalks, steps, doors and windows, seem to think our dusty line suffering by comparison, the many military looking men in these throngs watching the soldierly swing of our marching column with manifest though silent approval. And the Eleventh, with its one-armed Colonel riding at its head, its bullet tattered banners floating above it, and its men of '61, '62, '63, and '64 now welded by association, discipline and common danger into a compact if conglomerate mass, attracted no little attention as it kept step to the audacious declarations of its band—"That in Dixies land it took its stand to live and die in Dixies land." "Yes," drawled one ex-confederate officer to another, "they say this regiment was in the advance at Fair Oaks, McClellan's old boys ; none better." We went into camp in a grove back of the city. Here we remained for several months, doing such duty as was necessary in the militarily occupied city. From Richmond the "'62" men took their departure for Maine, the three years they had enlisted for having expired. The company was now officered by W. H. H. Frye as Captain, Nelson H. Norris as First Lieutenant, Lieutenant Perkins had become Captain of K, Lieutenant Young First Lieutenant of A, and First Sergeant Keene was made Second Lieutenant of H, a richly deserved honor, for there was no better soldier in the regiment than Josiah F. Keene. This reduced the "original members" remaining with the company to First Sergeant McGraw, Corporal Annis, Privates Day, Dunifer and Longley. The remainder of the company, now that the "'62" men were gone, being made up of the men of '63, who had joined the regiment at Gloucester Point, in April, 1864, and of the ones who had joined in the fall of 1864. On the 24th of November we were moved to Fredericksburgh, the headquarters of the military department known as that of Northeastern Virginia, then commanded by Brigadier-General Harris, but soon by Colonel Hill, for some time now Brevet Brigadier-General Hill. From here the companies were scattered through the department, D going to Northumberland County in what was called the sub-district of Essex. In January, 1866, the companies assembled at Fredericksburgh to go to City Point, where we were formally mustered out on the 2d of February, but we retained our company and regimental organization until we reached Augusta, where on the 10th day of February we were paid off, and Old Company D broke ranks for the last time.

The 26 in service at Muster-out of Regiment were :

CHARLES SELLMER, Capt. Co. B.
ALBERT MAXFIELD, Capt. Co. H.
ELLERY D. PERKINS, Capt. Co. K.
WM. H. H. FRYE, Capt. Co. D.
ROBERT BRADY, JR., 1st Lieut. Co. I.
NELSON H. NORRIS, 1st Lieut. Co. D.
JUDSON L. YOUNG, 1st Lieut. Co. A.
JOSIAH F. KEENE, 2d Lieut. Co. H.
TIMOTHY McGRAW, 1st Sergt.
STEPHEN MUDGETT, Sergt.
DANIEL W. WOODBURY, Sergt.
JOHN DEACON, Sergt.
FRANK E. YOUNG, Sergt.

JOTHAM S. ANNIS, Corporal.
ANDREW J. MUDGETT, Corporal.
JAMES E. DOW, Corporal.
FREDERICK ARNOLD, Private.
RUEL C. BURGESS, Private.
JOHN W. DAY, Private.
PRINCE E. DUNIFER, Private.
ALEXANDER B. DYER, Private.
HERVEY B. JOHNSON, Private.
LEONARD C. JUDKINS, Private.
JOHN LONGLEY, Private.
DENNIS TEHAN, Private.
JOSEPH VANDENBOSCH, Private.

1861   Roster of Company "D," Eleventh Regiment,   1890.

MAINE INFANTRY VOLUNTEERS.

†*See Personal Sketch.*

	AGE.	ENTERED SERVICE.	LEFT SERVICE.	HOW LEFT SERVICE.	RESIDENCE WHEN ENLISTED.	FINAL RECORD OR P O ADDRESS, 1890.	REMARKS.
CAPTAINS.							
1. Leonard S. Harvey..	30	Sept. 7, '61.	June 22, '62	Resigned.	Weston, Me.	San Francisco, Cal.	†Original Captain.
2. John D. Stanwood..	35	Sept. 12, '61.	Jan. 19, '63	"	Springfield, Me.	Winn, Me.	†Original First Lieutenant.
3. Albert G. Mudgett...	34	Sept. 25, '61.	May 13, '65.	Mustered out.	Newburg, Me	Greenleaf, Kansas.	†Prisoner at Bermuda Hundred, Va.
4. William H. H. Frye.	21	Nov. 7, '61.	Feb. 13, '66.	"	Fryeburg, Me.	Rosemont, Kansas.	†Promoted Brevet-Capt. U. S. Vols.
FIRST LIEUTENANTS.							
1. Leonard Butler......	21	July 18, '62.	Apr. 14, '63.	Died of Disease.	Hancock, Me	Died in Service.	†Died at Beaufort, S. C.
2. Charles Sellmer	31	June 13, '63.	Feb. 9, '66.	Mustered out	Beaufort, S. C.	Zollwood, Fla.	†Promoted Captain Co. B.
3. Albert Maxfield.....	25	Feb 27, '62.	Feb. 2, '66.	"	Windham, Me.	New York.	†Promoted Captain Co. H.
4. Ellery D. Perkins...	27	Aug. 16, '62.	Feb. 2, '66.	"	Cutler, Me.	Los Alamos, Cal.	†Promoted Captain Co. K.
5. Nelson H. Norris...	18	Oct 1, '61.	Feb. 2, '66.	"	Wayne, Me.	Aurora, Ills.	†Thrice Wounded.
SECOND LIEUTENANTS.							
1. Gibson S Badge....	26	Sept. 12, '61	Mar. 20, '62.	Resigned,	Springfield, Me.	Lee, Maine.	†Original Second Lieutenant.
2. Francis M. Johnson	31	Sept. 19, '61.	July 13, '63.	"	"	Springfield, Me.	†Prisoner at Mathews Co., Va.
3. Judson L. Young ..	23	Sept. 23, '61.	Feb. 2, 66	Mustered out.	"	Lincoln, Me.	†Promoted First Lieutenant Co. A.
FIRST SERGEANTS.							

SERGEANTS.

No.	Name	Age	Enlisted	Discharged	Disposition	Residence	Present Residence	Remarks
1.	James W. Noyes	25	Sept. 19, '61.	July 10, '62.	Died of Disease.	Topsfield, Me.	Died in Service.	Died in Baltimore, Md
2.	Ephriam Francis	33	Sept. 23, '61.	Nov. 18 '64	Mustered out.	Enfield, Me.	Bruce's Crossing. Mich.	†Mustered out at expiration of term.
3.	Gardiner E. Blake	33	July 17, '62.	Apr. 16, '65.	Disability.	Surry, Me.	W. Sullivan, Me.	†Prisoner at Bermuda Hundred, Va.
4.	Robert Brady, Jr.	16	Nov. 2, '61.	Feb. 2, '66.	Mustered out.	Enfield, Me.	New York.	†Promoted First Lieutenant Co. I.
5.	Alphonzo C. Gowell	18	Oct. 14 '61.	June 19, '65.	"	Litchfield, Me.	Hesperia, Mich.	†Prisoner at Hatcher's Run, Va
6.	Lyman M. Bragdon	24	July 17, '62.	June 12, '65.	"	Franklin, Me.	Franklin, Me.	†Wounded at Morris Island, S. C.
7.	Jeremiah Stratton	23	July 21, '62.	June 12, '65.	"	Hancock, Me.	Hancock, Me.	†Wounded at Hatcher's Run, Va.
8.	Stephen Mudgett	20	Dec 28, '63	Feb. 2, '66.	"	Newburg, Me.	Dixmont Centre, Me	Pro. Corp May 1, '65, Sergt June 1, '65
9.	Sumner E. Cushing	29	Aug 10, '63	Oct. 16, '65	"	Bangor, Me.	Thomaston. Me.	Pro. Corp June 1, '65, Sergt June 12 '65.
10.	Daniel W. Woolbury	18	July 15, '63	Feb. 2, '66.	"	Litchfield, Me.	"	†Wounded at Darbytown Road, Va.
11.	Joel Tucker	22	Oct. 12, '64.	Oct. 11, '65.	"	Millbridge, Me.	South China, Me.	Pro. Corp. June 12. '65. Sergt. July 1, '65.
12.	John Deacon	29	Dec 15, '64.	Feb. 2, '66	"	Portland, Me.		Pro. Corp. July 1, '65, Sergt Oct. 13, '65.
13.	Frank F. Young	21	Mar. 13, '65.	Feb. 2, '66.	"	Springfield, Me.	Drowned, June22, '80	†Drowned at Carson City, Col

CORPORALS

No.	Name	Age	Enlisted	Discharged	Disposition	Residence	Present Residence	Remarks
1	John McDonald	21	Sept 23, '61	May 16, '62.	Disability.	Topsfield, Me.	Calais, Me.	Discharged at Washington, D. C.
2	Richard W Dawe	27	Sept. 20, '61.	Apr. 20, '65.	Wounded.	"	Died Aug 11, '64	†Wounded at Bermuda Hundred, Va
3	Hughey G. Rideout	27	Sept. 9, '61.	Aug. 18, '62	Disability.	Springfield. Me.		†Discharged at Washington, D. C.
4	John Sherman	28	Sept. 23, '61.	Apr. 10, '62.	"	Topsfield, Me.	Lewiston, Me	Discharged at Washington, D. C
5	Benjamin Gould	23	Oct 12, '61.	Oct 3 '62.	"	Springfield, Me.		Discharged at Yorktown, Va.
6	Wm. H. Chamberlain	21	Oct. 24, '61.	Nov. 8, '62.	"	Enfield, Me.		Discharged at New York.
7	Ezra J. Philbrook	24	Sept 16, '61	Oct. 8, '62.	"	Springfield, Me.	Shelton, Neb.	Discharged at Washington, D. C.
8	Freeman R. Dakin	35	Sept. 28, '61.	Nov. 22, '62.	Disability.	Jackson Brook. Me.	Mulvane, Kas.	†Prisoner at Fair Oaks, Va.
9	John Gihn	26	Sept. 23, '61.	June 1, '63	"	Topsfield, Me.		†Discharged at Beaufort, S. C.
10.	Leonard M. Witham	28	Oct. 11, '61	Nov. 18, '62.	Died of Disease.	Enfield, Me.	Died in Service.	†Died at Yorktown, Va.
11.	Wm B Davis	45	Sept. 25, '61.	Sept. 23, '62.	Disability.	"	Died April 20, '87.	†Discharged at New York City.
12.	Nathan C. Messer	28	Sept. 24, '61.	Sept. 2, '62.	"	"	Lincoln, Me.	Discharged at Augusta, Me.
13.	James E. Bailey	18	Sept. 23, '61.	Dec 20, '64.	Wounded	Topsfield, Me.	Topsfield, Me	†Wounded at Bermuda Hundred, Va.
14.	Patrick Doherty	36	Sept. 17, '61.	Dec. 7, '62.	Disability.	Carroll, Me.	Died Sept. 16, '64	†Discharged at Yorktown, Va
15.	John Dyer	18	Sept 17, '61.	Nov 18, '64	Mustered out.	Springfield, Me	Killed May 23, '69.	†Killed at Springfield, Me.
16.	Horace Whittier	30	Aug. 27, '62	June 7, '65.	"	Haynesville, Me.	Glenwood, Me.	†Color Guard, wounded.
17.	Shepard Whittier	28	Aug. 27, '62.	June 28, '65.	"	Sidney, Me,	Campello, Mass.	†Color Guard.
18.	Stephen R. Bearce	27	Sept 23 '62	June 17, '65.	"	Carroll, Me.	Springfield, Me.	†Twice wounded.
19	Amaziah Hunter	24	Oct. 11, '61.	June 30, '65	"	Whitefield, Me.	E. Providence, R. I.	†Reenlisted First Sergeant Co. I.

	AGE.	ENTERED SERVICE.	LEFT SERVICE.	HOW LEFT SERVICE.	RESIDENCE WHEN ENLISTED.	FINAL RECORD OR P. O. ADDRESS, 1890.	REMARKS.
20. Wm. P. Weymouth.	30	Aug 15, '62.	Sept 2, '64	Died of Wounds.	Springfield, Me.	Died of Wounds.	†Twice wounded at Deep Bottom, Va.
21. James B Williams..	33	July 17, '62.	June 17, '65.	Mustered out.	Franklin, Me.	Drowned June 20, '81	‡Drowned at South West Harbor, Me
22. Alphonzo O. Donnell.	21	July 17, '62.	June 12, '65.	"	"		Promoted Corporal, Feb. 1, '65.
23. Edward Kennedy ...	20	Oct. 15, '64.	Oct 14, '65	"	Newry, Me.		Promoted Corporal, June 12, '65.
24. Samuel Ross......	32	Oct. 14, '64.	Oct. 13, '65.	"	Robbinston, Me.	N. Perry, Me.	Promoted Corporal, July 1, '65.
25. Jotham S. Annis....	39	Sept. 9, '61.	Feb, 2, '66.	"	Lee, Me.	Lee, Me	†Wounded at Drury's Bluff, Va.
26. Andrew J. Mudgett..	32	Dec. 28, '63.	Feb, 2, '66.	"	Newburgh, Me.	Jackson, Me.	Promoted Corporal, Oct 13, '65.
27. James E. Dow	23	July 6, '64.	Feb. 2, '66.	"	Bangor, Me.		Promoted Corporal, Oct. 13, '65.
MUSICIAN.							
1. Robert A. Strickland	18	Oct. 17, '61.	Apr. 20, '63	Disability	Gardiner, Me.	Bridgeport, Conn.	†Prisoner at Fair Oaks, Va.
WAGONERS.							
1 Henry W. Rider...	24	Sept. 20, '61	Feb 7, '62	Disability.	Bradford, Me	Died May 22, '64	†Discharged at Washington, D. C.
2. Wm. H. Hardison ..	27	July 22, '62.	Apr. 2, '65.	Died of Disease.	Franklin, Me.	Died in Service.	Died at Fortress Monroe, Va.
PRIVATES.							
1. Allen, George	18	Dec. 17, '63	July 15, '64	Died of Disease.	Linneus, Me.	Died in Service.	Died at Fortres Monroe, Va.
2. Arnold, Frederick ..	19	Dec 16, '64.	Feb. 2, '66.	Mustered out	Portland, Me.		M. O. with Regiment
3 Babb, Leonard P ...	19	Aug. 26, '62.	June 12, '65	"	Kennebunkport, Me	Died Feb 22, '71.	Died at Dover, N H.
4. Bartlett, Bartimus..	18	Sept. 30, '61.	Mar. 18, '62.	Died of Disease.	Lee, Me.	Died in Service.	Died at Washington, D. C.
5 Bartlett, Wm	19	Sept. 30, '61	Aug. 20 '62	Disability.	Lee, Me.		Discharged at Augusta, Me.
6 Bates, Thomas J ...	21	Oct. 9, '61.	Apr 8, '62.	Died of Disease.	Whitefield, Me.	Died in Service	Died at Newport News, Va.
7. Bearce, Philo	22	Sept. 10, '61.	July 14, '62	"	Springfield, Me.	"	Died at New York.
8. Betts, Bela W	43	Sept. 19, '61.	Aug 28, '62.	"	Weston, Me.	"	Died at Philadelphia, Pa.
9. Bickmore, Albion P..	18	Aug. 18, '64.	June 15, '65.	Mustered out.	Oldtown, Me.	Hyde Park, Mass.	Wd. and Pris at Hatcher's Run, Va., April 1, '65.
10 Blaine, Thomas R...	21	Feb. 18 '62	Feb. 28, '65	"	Frederickton, N. B.		Wd. at Fair Oaks, Va., May 31, '62.
11. Bolton, Sumner M..	32	Aug. 19, '63.	Apr. 1, '65.	Wounded.	Bangor, Me.	Bangor, Me.	†Wd. and Pris at Bermuda Hundred, Va.
12 Bragdon, Samuel A	19	July 21, '62	Aug 15, '64	Died of Wounds	Franklin, Me.	Died of Wounds.	†Twice Wounded.
13. Bridges, John E.....	18	Sept. 9, '61	June 2, '64.	Killed in Action.	Springfield, Me,	Killed in Action.	Killed at Bermuda Hundred, Va.

No.	Name	Age	Enlisted	Status	Date	Residence	Location	Remarks
14.	Bridgham, Leland F	20	Sept. 2, '63.	Mustered out.	June 5, '65.	Charleston Me.	Boston, Mass.	M. O at Baltimore, Md.
15.	Brien, Patrick	21	Aug 23 '64	"	"	Woodstock, N. B.		Pris. at Hatcher's Run Va., April 1, '65.
16.	Brown, John	21	Dec. 7, '64	Deserted.	Aug 10, '65	Sherbrook, N. S.		Deserted at Richmond, Va.
17.	Bryant, James W.	21	Aug. 23, '62	Mustered out.	June 12, '65	Springfield, Me.	N. Lee, Me.	M O at Richmond, Va.
18.	Bryant, Martin V.	21	Aug. 8, '62	"	Oct. 3, '65.	Hermon, Me.	N Carmel, Me.	M O at Richmond, Va.
19.	Buhier, Frank	19	Aug. 25, '63	Died of Wounds.	Sept. 13, '64	Lewiston, Me.	Died of Wounds.	†Prisoner at Bermuda Hundred, Va
20	Burgess, Ruel C.	23	Aug 1, '63	Mustered out.	Feb. 2, '66.	Vassalboro, Me.	N. Vassalboro, Me.	Wounded at Deep Run, Va., Aug, 16, '64.
21.	Burke, Charles H.	18	Sept 28, '61	Disability.	April 5, '62.	Lee, Me.	Lee, Me.	M. O. with Regiment.
22.	Burns, John	23	Dec. 16, '64.	Mustered out.	Dec 19 '65.	Limington, Me.	W. Oakland, Cal	Discharged at Washington, D. C.
23.	Buswell, Silas. Jr.	24	Sept. 24, '61.	Disability.	April 14. '62.	Enfield, Me	Antigo, Wis	Wounded at Appomattox, Va, April 9, '65
24.	Butler, Alfred C.	21	Feb. 29, '64.	Wounded.	Sept 19, '65.	Eastbrook, Me.	Waltham, Me.	Discharged at Washington, D. C.
25.	Butler, Geo. L.	24	July 23 '62	Died of Wounds.	May 20, '64.	"	Died of Wounds.	†Thrice Wounded at Deep Bottom, Va.
26.	Butterfield, Geo. M	18	Sept. 16, '61.	Disability.	July 28, '62	Springfield, Me.	Springfield, Me.	†Wd. at Bermuda H'lred, Va., May 17, '64.
27.	Buzzell, Wm A	30	Sept 30, '61.	"	April 28, '62	Enfield, Me	Died Nov. 16, '62.	Discharged at Harrison's Landing, Va.
28.	Cain, Henry H.	21	July 30, '63.	"	Sept 10, '65.	Vassalboro, Me.	Jacksonville, Vt.	Discharged at Yorktown, Va,
29.	Cannavan, John.	21	Oct 11, '64	"	Oct. 11, '65	Portland, Me.		†Discharged at Washington, D. C.
30.	Carlow, John P.	31	Oct 3. '64.	Mustered out.	May 25, '65	Wesley, Me.		M. O. at Richmond, Va.
31.	Carver, Alonzo	18	Oct 9, '61.	"	Nov. 15 '64.	Lee, Me		M. O. at Richmond, Va
32.	Cilley, Clark	36	Sept. 30, '61.	Disability.	Dec. 17, '62	Springfield, Me	Stacyville, Me.	Wd. at Bermuda H'ldred, Va., May 17, '64.
33.	Clark, Samuel S	25	July 17, '62.	Mustered out.	Aug. 14, '65.	Franklin, Me.	Springfield, Me.	Discharged at Washington, D. C.
34.	Cline, Joseph	28	July 28, '62	Died of Disease.	Dec. 9, '62.	Hancock, Me.	Franklin, Me.	Promoted Fife Major, Nov. 18, '64.
35.	Collins, Francis	21	July 17, '62.	Wounded.	Mar. 23 '65.	Franklin, Me.		Died at Yorktown, Va
36.	Collins, Josiah	28	Oct. 8, '61.	Disability.	Mar. 28, '62.	Springfield. Me.	Died Dec. 25, '77.	Wd. at Deep Bottom, Va., Aug, 14, '64.
37.	Conforth, Melvin.	21	Sept. 9 '61.	Mustered out.	Nov. 18, '64.	"	Minneapolis, Minn.	†Discharged at Washington, D. C.
38.	Cook, Joseph	35	Oct. 18, '61.	"		Levant, Me.		Wd. at Bermuda H'lred, Va., June 2, '64.
39.	Cooper, Geo. L.	32	Sept. 30, '61.	Died of Disease.	May 15, '62.	Springfield, Me.	Died in Service,	Died at New York City.
40.	Cooper, Hiram A.	23	Sept 30, '61.	Disability.	April 1, '62.	Prentiss, Me.	N. Newport, Me.	Discharged at Washington, D. C.
41.	Cote, George	23	Dec. 12, '64	Mustered out.	Dec. 16, '65.	Oldtown, Me.	Burling Falls, N. H.	M. O. at Richmond, Va.
42.	Crabtree, Isaac N.	37	July 17, '62.	Disability.	Nov. 27, '62.	Franklin, Me	E. Sullivan, Me.	Discharged at Washington, D. C.
43.	Cronin, Daniel	22	July 29, '62.	Died of Disease.	Oct. 31, '62.	Eastbrook, Me.	Died in Service.	Died at Yorktown, Va.
44.	Crosby, Thomas A.	23	Aug. 5, '63.	"	Aug. 27, '64.	Swanville, Me.	"	Died at Point-of-Rocks, Va.
45.	Cross, Simon	40	Sept. 20, '61.	Disability.	Mar. 26, '62.	Topsfield, Me.	Died Feb. 5, '64.	Died at Point-of-Rocks, Va.
46.	Curtis, Elijah B.	18	Sept 30, '61.	"	Mar. '62.	Enfield, Me.	Died June 12, '62.	"
47.	Curtis, John T.	22	Aug. 5, '63.	Mustered out.	May 29, '65	Byron, Me.	Boston, Mass.	Wd. at Appomattox, Va, April 9, '65.
48.	Curtis, Phineas	42	Sept. 30, '61.	Died of Disease.	July '62	Enfield, Me.	Died in Service,	Died at Yorktown, Va.

		AGE	ENTERED SERVICE.	LEFT SERVICE.	HOW LEFT SERVICE.	RESIDENCE WHEN ENLISTED.	FINAL RECORD OR P. O. ADDRESS, 1890	REMARKS.
49.	Darling, Wm H...	22	Sept. 25, '61.	Nov. 18, '64.	Mustered out.	Enfield, Me.	Enfield, Me.	M. O. at Augusta, Me.
50.	Davis, John F....	18	Sept. 7, '61.	May 26, '62.	Died of Disease.	Chelsea, Me.	Died in Service.	Died at Baltimore, Md.
51.	Davis, Thomas A..	19	Sept. 7, '61.	'63	Disability.	Whitefield, Me.	Killed Sept. 27, '64	†On Gunboat Service, Feb 17, '62.
52.	Day, John W	31	Sept. 9, '61.	Feb. 9, '66	Mustered out.	Springfield, Me.	Springfield. Me.	Wd. at Deep Run, Va., Aug. 16, '64.
53.	Dolly, Charles ...	24	Sept. 11, '61.	Dec 18, '61.	Died of Disease	" "	Died in Service	Died at Washington, D. C.
54.	Downs Charles....	20	Sept. 30, '61.	May 9, '63	Disability	" "	Springfield, Me.	Dis. at Hilton Head, S. C.
55.	Driscoll, John H...	21	July 18, '62.	June 12, '65.	Mustered out.	Franklin, Me.	Cherryfield, Me.	M. O. at Richmond, Va.
56.	Dunifer, Prince E..	26	Sept. 9, '61.	Feb 9, '66.	" "	Springfield, Me.	Winn, Me.	M. O. at Augusta, Me.
57.	Dyer, Alexander B.	23	Feb. 22, '64.	Feb 2, '66.	" "	Eastbrook, Me.	Franklin, Me.	Served also in Co. C, 26th Me
58.	Dyer, Geo E.	29	July 17, '62.	Jan. 16, '63.	Disability.	Franklin, Me.	Died '63	Died at Franklin, Me.
59.	Dyer, Hudson K ..	22	Feb. 22, '64.	Feb 9, '65.	Died of Disease.	Eastbrook, Me	Died in Service	Wd. at Bermuda Hundred, Va , June 2, '64.
60.	Ellis, Daniel S ...	18	Sept. 16, '61.	Aug 18, '62.	Disability.	Springfield, Me.		Dis at Augusta, Me.
61.	Findel, Wm H....	24	Oct 12, '64	June 20, '65.	Mustered out	E. Machias, Me.	Barrington, N. S.	Pris. at Hatchers Run, Va., April 1, '65
62.	Fogg, Geo M	18	Oct. 15, '61.	May 15, '63	Died of Disease.	Lowell, Me.	Died in Service.	Died at Beaufort, S. C.
63.	Folsom Jeremiah..	48	Oct. 9, '61.	Mar. 26, '62.	Disability.	Burlington, Me.	Died.	Dis at Washington, D. C.
64.	Foss, Augustus I...	24	July 24, '62.	Mar. 7, '63	Died of Disease	Hancock, Me.	Died in Service.	Died at Hilton Head, S. C.
65.	Foss, Charles M ...	21	Sept 16, '61.	Sept. 2, '62	Disability.	Lee, Me		Dis. at Augusta, Me.
66.	Freeman, Geo. L...	19	Sept. 9, '61.	Dec. 16, '61.	Died of Disease.	Vassalboro, Me.	Died in Service.	Died at Washington, D. C.
67.	Frost, Stephen.....	26	Sept. 30, '61.	June 8, '62	Deserted	Prentiss, Me		Deserted at Bottom's Bridge, Va.
68.	Geary, George ...	24	Oct. 10, '64.	May 24, '65.	Mustered out.	Baldwin, Me.		Pris. at Hatchers Run, Va., April 1, '65.
69.	Gerry, Geo. H....	18	Sept 9, '61.	Aug 18, '62.	Disability.	Springfield, Me	S. H. Togus, Me.	Dis. at Augusta, Me.
70.	Getchell, Isaac J...	42	Oct 4. '64	June 24, '65.	Mustered out	Millbridge, Me.	Millbridge, Me.	Dis. at York, Pa.
71.	Gibbs, Elisha W...	23	Aug. 23, '63.	June 19, '65.	" "	Oldtown, Me.	Died May 24, '78.	†Pris. at Hatchers Run, Va., April 1, '65.
72.	Googing, Amaziah T	19	July 18, '62.	Jan. 23, '63.	Disability.	Hancock, Me.	Cornell, Ills.	Dis at Yorktown, Va. [Arm Amp
73.	Gouging, Augustus N	18	July 18, '02.	Nov. 19, '64.	Wounded.	" "	Died Aug 16, '70.	Wd. at Deep Run, Va., Aug 16, '64. Left
74.	Gould, Ira	20	Sept. 10, '61.	Aug. 18, '62.	Disability.	Springfield, Me.	Caribou, Me.	Dis. at Augusta, Me,
75.	Gray, Daniel.......	26	Oct. 16, '61.	May 31, '62.	Missing in action	Enfield, Me.	Probably killed.	†Missing at Battle of Fair Oaks, Va.
76.	Hall, John	28	Aug. 4, '63.	Aug. 14 '64	Killed in action	Lewiston, Me.	Killed in action	Killed at Deep Bottom Va.
77.	Hanscom, Elbridge E	22	Sept. 30, '61.	Aug. 16, '64	" "	Topsfield, Me.	" "	Killed at Deep Run, Va.
78.	Harrington, Cornelius	23	Oct. 17, '64.	Oct 18, '65.	Mustered out	New Bedford, Mass.	New Bedford, Mass	M. O. at Richmond, Va.
79.	Hayden, Greenlief .	40	Oct. 7, '61.	Mar. 27, '62.	Died of Disease	Skowhegan, Me.	Died in Service.	Died at Washington, D. C.
80.	Haegan, Ira B......	26	July 18, '62.	July 11, '65.	Mustered out.	Hancock, Me.	N. Lamoine, Me.	†M. O. at New York.
81.	Haegan, Peter D....	21	July 21, '62.	June 12, '65.	" "	Sullivan, Me	Died Sept. 3. '85.	Died at Franklin, Me
82.	Hooper, Amaziah C.	25	July 17, '62.	June 12. '65.	" "	Franklin, Me.	Franklin, Me.	M. O. at Richmond, Va

No.	Name	Age	Enlisted	Date	Cause	Town	Later	Remarks
83.	House, Mathew P ..	18	Sept 13, '61.	Nov. 18, '64.	" "	Lee, Me.		†Pris. at Fair Oaks, Va
84	Hunton, Napoleon B	21	Aug 13, '63.	June 26, '65.	Mustered out.	Milford, Me	Minneapolis, Minn.	M. O. at Augusta, Me.
85	Hutchinson, Eleazer	19	Sept. 14, '61.	April 1, '62.	Disability.	Lincoln, Me.	Shelton, Wash.	†Discharged at Washington, D. C
86	Jackman, Adolphus O	23	Sept. 20, '61.	Aug 11, '62.	"	Topsfield, Me.	S. II. Dayton, O.	Discharged at Augusta, Me.
87.	Johnson, Hervey B	19	Aug 25, '64.	Feb. 2, '66	Mustered out.	Sanford, Me.		M. O with Regiment.
88.	Judkins, Leonard C.	22	July 15, '63.	Feb. 2, '66.	" "	Lewiston, Me.		M. O. with Regiment.
89	Kelley, Lawrence..	29	Aug. 15, '63.	Sept. 9, '64.	Died of Disease	Eaton Grant, Me.	Died in Service.	†Died in Andersonville Prison, Ga
90.	Laflin, Pierce	19	July 18, '62.	July 31, '65.	Mustered out.	Hancock, Me	Truckee, Cal	†Wd. at Morris Island, S. C., Dec. 25, '63
91	Lampson, John A	26	July 18, '64.	May 9, '63.	Disability.	Franklin, Me.	Ellsworth, Me.	Discharged at Hilton Head, S. C
92	Lancaster, Sam'l B	28	Aug. 15, '62	June 12, '65;	Mustered out.	Springfield, Me.	Montague, Me.	M. O at Richmond, Va.
93	Lane, Otis	36	Nov. 9, '63.	Jan. 10, '65.	Wounded.	Biddeford, Me.	Died June 18, '70	†Wd. at Bermuda Hundred, Va
94	Leighton, Leonard S.	40	Sept. 30, '61.	July 17, '65	"	Springfield, Me.	Died April 12, '86.	†Wd. at Deep Run, Va., Aug 16, '64
95.	Longely, John	28	Sept, 23, '61.	Feb. 2, '66	Mustered out.	Orono, Me.	Died Jan. 25, '73	Died at Orono, Me.
96.	Lowell, Charles A...	23	Sept. 30, '61.	Jan. 17, '62	Died of Disease.	Springfield, Me	Died in Service	Died at New York
97.	Lunt, Joseph W	36	Oct. 24, '64.	Nov 4, '65	Mustered out.	Long Island Pl., Me.	Swan's Island, Me.	M. O. at Fortress Monroe, Va.
98	Maddox, Greenlief	32	Aug 18, '62	June 12, '65	" "	Kennebunkport, Me.	Lyman, Me	†Wd. at Morris Island, S. C., Dec. 8, '63
99	Malkson, Daniel F	19	Sept 30, '61	Dec. 27, '64.	Died of Disease.	Topsfield, Me	Died in Service.	Died at Fortress Monroe, Va.
100	Malkson, George ..	21	Sept. 23, '61.	May 9 '63.	Disability.	" "	Elk River, Minn	Discharged at Hilton Head, S C.
101	Malkson, Wm V...	45	Sept 25, '61.	Jan 15, '62.	"	" "	Topsfield, Me.	Discharged at Washington, D. C.
102	Mathews, Robert....	22	Aug. 18, '64	July 12, '65	Mustered out.	Eastport, Me.	Eastport, Me.	Wd at Hatcher's Run, Va., April 2, '65
103	McCormick, Wm...	22	Oct 4, '64	Nov. 6, '64.	Deserted.	St Johns, N. B.		De-erted at New York
104	McKenney, Simeon S	27	Oct. 12, '61	Nov. 3, '62.	Disability.	Enfield, Me.	Lincoln, Neb	Discharged at Providence, R. I.
105	McPhetres, John V	18	Oct. 12, '61	June 6, '62.	Died of Disease.	Lowell, Me.	Died in Service.	Died at Bottoms Bridge, Va
106.	Merrill Charles H	23	Aug. 13, '63	May 11, '65.	Disability.	Lee, Me.	Lee, Me.	Discharged at Augusta. Me.
107	Morrill, Charles F.	18	Sept. 17, '63	May 29, '65	Mustered out.	Corinna, Me.	Killed April 6 '82.	†Wd. at Hatcher's Run, Va., April 2, '65
108.	Morris, John......	28	Oct. 18, '64.	June 5, '65	" "	Naples, Me.	S. H. Togus, Me.	M. O at Fortress Monroe, Va.
109	Mullen, Guy.......	25	July 18, '62.	June 1, '63.	Disability.	Hancock, Me.	N. Hancock, Me.	Discharged at Beaufort, S. C.
110	Murdough, James...	18	Sept. 20, '61.	June 1, '62	Died of Disease.	Albion, Me	Died in Service.	Died at Yorktown, Va.
111.	Newell, Loren......	27	Oct. 31, '64	Nov. 10, '65	Mustered out.	Gardiner, Me	Died in Service.	M. O. at Richmond, Va.
112	Norton, James C...	22	Aug. 15, '62.	Oct 31, '62.	Died of Disease.	Springfield, Me.	Died in Service.	Died at Yorktown, Va.
113	Norton, Thomas....	20	Aug 15, '62	Mar. 17, '63	Disability.	" "	Rice's Station, Minn.	Dis-charged at Hilton Head, S C.
114.	Orcutt, Asa D	44	July 30, '62.	Dec. 19, '62,	" "	Franklin, Me.	Died Dec 24, '62	Discharged at Yorktown, Va.
115.	Parsons, Charles L.	18	Oct. 12, '64.	Nov. 5, '65.	Dis. by order.	E. Machias, Me.	Machias, Me.	Discharged at Richmond, Va.
116.	Philbrook, Charles	18	Aug. 15, '62	Nov. 26, '62	Died of Disease	Springfield, Me.	Died in Service.	Died at Yorktown, Va
117.	Philbrook, David C	28	Sept. 2, '61.	Sept. 15, '62.	Disability.	" "	Died Aug , '64.	†Discharged at Yorktown, Va.
118.	Philbrook, Jeremiah	44	Sept 7, '61.	June 17, '62.	"	" "	Died June 18, '86	Discharged at Washington, D. C.
119	Robinson, George..	33	Sept. 17, '61	Nov. 22, '62.	Died of Disease	Lee, Me.	Died in Service.	Died at Yorktown, Va.

		Age.	Entered Service.	Left Service.	How Left Service.	Residence When Enlisted.	Final Record or P O Address, 1890.	Remarks.
120.	Ryan, Otis W	33	Nov. 11, '64	Apr. 2, '65.	Died of Wounds.	Knox, Me.	Died of Wounds.	Wd. at Hatchers Run, Va., Apr. 2, '65.
121.	Seavey, George	21	Oct. 25, '64	June 4, '65.	Mustered out.	Gorham, Me.		Pris. at Hatchers Run, Va., Apr. 1, '65.
122.	Shaw, Le Baron H	31	Aug. 15, '62.	Dec. 5, '62.	Disability.	Springfield, Me.	Moro, Me.	Dis. at Yorktown, Va.
123.	Shepard, Geo. M	21	Sept. 9, '61.	Apr. 1, '62.	"	"	Springfield, Me.	Dis. at Washington, D. C.
124.	Shepard, Harvey C	18	Sept. 8, '61.	Aug. 14, '64.	Killed in action.	"	Killed in action.	Killed at Deep Bottom, Va.
125.	Sherman, Moses E.	24	Sept. 23, '61.	Apr. 9, '65.	"	Topsfield, Me.	"	†Killed at Appomattox, Va.
126.	Sherman, Wm	22	Sept. 10, '61.	Sept. 1, '64	Died of Wounds.	Carroll, Me	Died of Wounds.	†Wd. at Deep Bottom, Va., Aug 14, '64.
127.	Sibley, Adoniram	18	Sept. 19, '61.	May 9, '63.	Disability.	Lowell, Me.	Died Feb. 8, '81.	Dis. at Hilton Head, S. C.
128.	Sibley, Sumner	26	Sept. 9, '61	Apr. 1, '62.	"	"	Died Mar. 28, '63	Dis. at Washington, D. C.
129.	Simmonds, James	43	Oct. 17, '64.	May 24, '65.	Mustered out.	Calais, Me.	Died.	Pris. at Hatchers Run, Va., Apr. 1, '65.
130.	Smith, Wm P.	18	Dec. 5, '64.	Dec. 20, '65.	Disability.	Prospect, Me.	Waldo, Me.	
131.	Smith, Zelman, B.	19	July 31 '62.	May 18, '65.	Dis. by order.	Eastbrook, Me.	Ingalls, Mich.	Wd. at Bermuda Hundred, Va., June 2, '64.
132.	Spaulding, Samuel H	23	Sept. 30, '62.	June 12, '65.	Mustered out.	Springfield, Me.	Lakeville, Me.	M. O. at Richmond, Va.
133.	Sprague, Darius D.	27	Oct. 3, '64.	Oct. 3, '65.	"	Millbridge, Me.	Millbridge, Me.	M. O. at Richmond, Va.
134.	Sprague, Volney	18	Sept. 17, '63.	Aug, 17, '65.	Disability.	Corinna, Me.	Lowell, Mass.	
135.	Stanley, John N.	20	Sept 16, '61.	Aug. 14, '64	Killed in action.	Prentiss, Me.	Killed in action.	Killed at Deep Bottom, Va , Aug. 14, '64.
136.	Stanely, Rufus D.	29	Feb. 10, '62	Dec. 12, '62.	Disability.	"	Prentiss, Me.	Dis. at New Haven, Ct.
137.	Staples, Wentworth	26	Sept. 26, '61.	July 7, '62.	"	Lee, Me.	Lincoln, Me.	Dis. at Philadelphia, Pa.
138.	Starbird, Chas. D.	26	July 15, '63.	Nov. 20, '65	Wounded.	Litchfield, Me.	Died May 22, '87.	Wd. at Deep Bottom. Va., Aug. 14, '64.
139.	Sterling, John	25	Dec. 12, '64.	Mar. 14, '65.	Transferred.	Liverpool, C. B.		Returned to 4th Mass. Cavalry.
140.	Stevens John T.	21	Oct. 8, '64.	June 19, '65.	Mustered out.	Bangor, Me.	Greenville, Me.	Pris. at Hatchers Run, Va., Apr 1, '65.
141.	Stewart, Asa L.	19	July 17, '62	Nov. 13, '62.	Died of Disease.	Franklin, Me.	Died in Service.	Died at Yorktown, Va.
142.	Stratton, Adelbert.	26	July 24, '62.	Aug 15, '64.	Died of Wounds.	Hancock, Me.	Died of Wounds.	Wd. at Deep Bottom, Va., Aug 14, '64
143.	Sweet, Joseph	22	Dec. 14, '64.	July 7, '62.	Died of Disease.	Topsfield, Me.	Died in Service.	Died at Portsmouth Grove, R. I
144.	Tehan, Dennis	21	Oct. 13, '64.	Feb. 2, '66.	Mustered out.	Machiasport, Me.	Newport, Ky.	Wd. at Hatchers Run, Va., Mar 31, '65
145.	Tibbetts, Jeremiah.	32	Dec. 22, '61.	Oct. 13, '65.	"	Columbia, Me.	Died Apr. 27, '74.	M. O. at Richmond, Va.
146.	Vandenbosch, Joseph	22	Dec. 22, '64.	Feb. 2, '66.	"	Boothbay, Me.		M. O. with Regiment.
147.	Versteylen, Jacob.				"	"		
148.	Von Siebold, Alex't.	37	Aug 28, '63	May 30, '65.	"	Boston, Mass.		Prom. Sergt. Maj., Nov. 18, '64. Wd. Apr. [9, '65.
149.	Watson, Geo. W .	19	Sept. 19, '64.	May 8, '65.	Died of Wounds.	Emblen, Me.	Died of Wounds.	Wd. at Hatchers Run, Va Apr. 2, 65. Died at [Point of Rocks.
150	Welch, Fred M.	24	Aug. 16, '62.	July 10, '65.	Mustered out.	Kennebunkport, Me.	Saco, Me.	Trans to V.R.C. Feb 18, '64
151.	Welch, Wm. P .	27	Aug. 16, '62	Oct. 27, '62.	Died of Disease.	"	Died in Service.	Died at Yorktown, Va
152.	White, Geo. O.	27	Aug, 6, '63.	June 14, '65.	Wounded.	Belmont, Me.	Monroe, Me.	Wl at Deep Run, Va , Aug, 16, '64.
153.	Woodman, Hiram A	20	Sept. 24, '61.	Nov 18, '64.	Mustered out.	Springfield, Me		†M. O. at Expiration of Term.
154	Wosler, Alfred	18	Sept. 20 '61.	Mar 25, '64	Deserted	No 7, R. 2. Me.		Deserted at Augusta, Me.

PERSONAL SKETCHES.

Captain Leonard S. Harvey entered service as Captain, and resigned soon after the Regiment entered active service.

Captain John D. Stanwood entered service as 1st Lietenant. He commanded Co. D, from July, '62, until December, '62, and resigned on account of ill health January 19, '63.

Captain Albert G. Mudgett entered service as 2d Lieutenant of Co. K, was promoted 1st Lieutenant of Co. G, December 1, '62, Captain Co. D, June 13, '63, was taken prisoner at Bermuda Hundred, Va., June 2, '64, and was a prisoner until the close of the war.

Captain Wm. H. H. Frye entered service as Corporal, in Co. A, was promoted Sergeant, October 3, '62, discharged for disability December 18, '62, reenlisted Private in Co. A, November 17, '63, was promoted 1st Sergeant March 4, '64, was wounded severely in leg at Deep Run, Va., August 16, '64, commissioned 2d Lieutenant Co. B, August 16, '64, but not mustered, promoted 1st Lieutenant Co. C, December 13, '64, and Captain Co. D, June 23, '65. During the spring campaign of 1865, Lieutenant Frye served on the staff of Major-General R. S. Foster, commanding 1st division, 24th A. C. and did gallant and meritorious service in the pursuit of Lee's Army from Petersburg to Appomattox, for which he was promoted Brevet-Captain of U. S. Vols. by the President. When the regiment was ordered to the N. E. District of Va. Captain Frye was assigned to duty in the sub-district of Essex, as Provost-Marshal and Assistant Superintendent of Freedmen, in the Counties of Northumberland and Westmoreland, Va., where he served until ordered to be mustered out.

Lieutenant Leonard Butler entered service as 2d Lieutenant of Co. H. He was promoted 1st Lieutenant Co D, November 1, '62. He commanded Co. D from December '62 to April 14, '63.

Col. Chas. Sellmer joined Co. D as 1st Lieutenant, June 13, 1863, from 1st Sergeant Battery D 1st U. S. Artillery, in which he had served from November 8, 1854, to date of joining 11th Maine. During these nine years he served in Fla., (taking part in second Seminole War,) Va., La., and S. C., and was present at surrender of Baton Rouge Arsenal to the State of Louisiana in February, 1861, declining splendid offers made him if joining the Southern Cause. Lieutenant Sellmer acted as instructor of Artillery to the 11th Maine, and as A. A. I. G. District of Amelia Island until ordered to command a detachment of 40 men from Co's C, E, G & K, 11th Maine to serve as artillerists on Morris Island, S. C., during the siege of Charleston and Fort Wagner, manning mortar batteries and the famous "Swamp Angel," which fired the first shell into the city. Upon the organization of the "Army of the James" he was appointed A. A. I. G. 3d

Brig. 1st Div. 10th A. C. and A. A. I. G. 1st Div. 10th A. C. December 1864. Promoted Captain Co. B, July 17, 1864. Captain Sellmer served on the staff of Major-General R. S. Foster, commanding 1st Div. 24th A. C. during the winter of 1864, to July, 1865, and as A. A. I. G. of Dept. Va. from that time to muster out of the regiment. He was breveted Major for "conspicuous gallantry in the assault on Fort Gregg, Va.," and Lieutenant–Colonel for "gallant and meritorious services during the war." He was in the field from the surrender of Baton Rouge Arsenal, La. 1861, until the war ended with Lee's surrender, was twice wounded, though never reported officially. Appointed 2d Lieutenant U. S. Army September 2d, 1867. Graduated at the U. S. Artillery School at Fortress Monroe, Va., in 1872. Promoted 1st Lieutenant, 3d Artillery, July 2d, 1877, which position he holds to date, (a Lieutenant for 23 years,) with no hope for promotion before his retirement by operation of law in 1896. During his 23 years service as a commissioned officer of the regular army, he has served in almost every capacity—Commissary of Subsistence, Quartermaster, Adjutant, Ordnance Officer, Post Treasurer, Recruiting Officer, Battery Commander of heavy and light Artillery Batteries in almost every State of the Union.

Captain Albert Maxfield entered service as Private in Co. C, was promoted Commissary Sergeant of the Regiment, January 3, '63. Reenlisted February 29, '64. Promoted Sergeant-Major March 1, '64, 2d Lieutenant Co. D, May 10, '64, 1st Lieutenant Co. D, July 18, '64, and Captain Co. H, December 17, '64. Lieutenant Maxfield commanded Co. D, from June 2, '64 to July 28, '64 and from August 29, '64 to December 21, '64. He was slightly wounded October 7, '64. He commanded the regiment from November 2, '64, until after the Presidential Election, the Eleventh being one of the regiments selected by Major-General B. F. Butler to assist in keeping the peace in New York City during the election. In the campaign in pursuit of Lee's Army from Petersburg to Appomattox, there being but one field officer on duty with the regiment, Captain Maxfield was assigned to the command of the left wing. He was taken prisoner at Appomattox, went to Annapolis, was declared exchanged May 1, '65 and returned to the regiment. He was member of a Court-Martial at Headquarters 1st division 24th A. C. while the regiment was at Chapin's Farm, and also at camp of 20th N. Y. S. M. in the summer of '65. When the regiment was ordered to the N. E. District of Va. he was given command of the Sub-District of Essex, comprising the counties of Essex, Middlesex, King and Queen, Lancaster, Richmond, Westmoreland and Northumberland, with Headquarters at Tappahannock, where he remained until ordered to be mustered out.

Captain Ellery D. Perkins was the son of James Perkins, who served in the war of 1812, a musician in the 17th U. S. Infantry. Captain Perkins entered service a Private in Co. B, he was promoted Sergeant September 8, '62, Commissary-Sergeant of the regiment March 1,'64, 2d Lieutenant Co. D, July 19, '64, 1st Lieutenant Co. D, December 18, '64, and Captain Co. K, April 16, '65. Lieutenant Perkins acted R. Q. M. from November 1, '64 to November 30, '64,

Commanded Co. F, from December 1, '64 to December 21, '64. Commanded Co. D from December 21, '64 to February, '65, and from March, '65 to April 16, '65. Commanded Co. K, from April 16, '65, until mustered out of service. When the regiment was ordered to the Northeastern District of Va., he was assigned to duty as Provost-Marshal and Assistant Superintendent of Freedmen for Rappahannock County, with Headquarters at the village of Washington, and later was appointed Provost-Marshal of the District of N. E. Va., on the staff of Brevet Brigadier-General J. A. Hill, commanding the district with Headquarters at Fredericksburg, which position he held until ordered to City Point, Va., to be mustered out.

Lieutenant Nelson H. Norris entered service as Private in Co. F, was wounded at Fair Oaks, Va., May 31, '62, was promoted Hospital Steward, November 22, '62, resigned warrant and was transferred to Co. C as Private, May 1, '64, was wounded at Strawberry Plains, Va., July 26, '64, was promoted 2d Lieutenant of Co. B, August 13, '64, was wounded at Hatcher's Run, Va., April 2, '65, was promoted 1st Lieutenant Co. D, April 16, '65. During the summer of '65, was member of a Court-Martial at the camp of the 20th N. Y. S. M., and when the regiment was ordered to the Northeastern District of Va. he was Act. Assistant Adjutant-General of the Sub-District of Essex, and afterwards Post Q. M. at Tappahannock, Va., until ordered to City Point, Va., to be mustered out. After leaving service he studied medicine and graduated at Dartmouth College, in '67, since which he has practised in Maine, Wisconsin and for the last 12 years in Illinois.

Lieutenant Gibson S. Budge entered service as 2d Lieutenant. He resigned on account of disability before the regiment left Washington.

Lieutenant Francis M. Johnson entered service as Sergeant, was promoted 2d Lieutenant, March 18, '62. He commanded Co. D from June 22, '62 until after the Seven Days Battles before Richmond and until after the regiment arrived at Harrison's Landing, also from April 14, '63, to June, '63. He was taken prisoner in Mathews County, Va., November 24, '62.

Lieutenant Judson L. Young entered service as Sergeant, reenlisted January 16, '64, was wounded at Deep Run, Va., August 18, '64, was promoted 1st Sergeant, September 16, '64, 2d Lieutenant December 18, '64, and 1st Lieutenant Co. A, April 25, '65. As Sergeant, he acted 1st Sergeant from May 31, '62, to November, '62, and from July 15, '63, to July 10, '64. As Lieutenant he commanded Co. D from February, '65 to March, '65, and from April 16, '65 to June 12, '65, when he took command of Co. A, which command he retained until mustered out. When the regiment was ordered to the N. E. District of Va., Lieutenant Young was assigned to duty as Provost-Marshal and Assistant Superintendent of Freedmen for Fauquier County, with Headquarters at Warrenton, and later was Provost-Marshal and Assistant Superintendent of Freedman for Spotsylvania County, holding alternate sessions of the Freedman's Court at Spotsylvania C. H. and the City of Fredericksburg.

Lieutenant Robert Brady entered service as 1st Sergeant, was taken prisoner at Fair Oaks, Va., May 31, '62, and was confined in Libby Prison, at Prison in Saulsbury, N. C., and at Belle Isle in the James River opposite Richmond, until November, '62, when he was paroled and sent to Annapolis, Md., until declared exchanged, when he returned to the regiment, then at Yorktown, Va., he was promoted 2d Lieutenant Co. B, October 1, '62, transferred to Co. G Nov. 19, '62, and resigned on account of impaired health, March 14, '63.

1st Sergeant Abner F. Bassett entered service as Sergeant, was promoted 1st Sergeant November 1, '62. He was taken prisoner at Fair Oaks, ·Va., May 31, '62, and was a prisoner with 1st Sergeant Brady and others until Nov., '62, when he returned to the regiment. He was on recruiting service at Portland, Me., from Aug. 15, '63, to July 10, '64. He was killed on the picket line in front of Petersburgh, Va., Sept. 15, '64, and was buried on the 16th, near our camp, "amid the booming of cannon and whistling of bullets"—so reads the entry made in the diary of Sergeant-Major Morton.

Lieutenant Josiah F. Keene entered service as Private, was promoted Corporal May 16, '62. At the Battle of White Oaks Swamp, June 30, '62, he acted as Orderly to Colonel H. M. Plaisted, commanding the regiment, and several times volunteered to advance beyond the skirmish line to a point where he could observe any attempt on the part of the enemy to cross the swamp· Here also he discovered and recovered the three horses tied to a tree, between the lines, belonging to officers of the Union Army, to which Colonel P. refers in his report to the Adjutant-General of Maine. For his coolness and services during the battle he was highly complimented by Colonel Plaisted.

He was taken prisoner in Matthews Co., Va., Nov. 24, '62, and was paroled from Libby Prison and exchanged. Reenlisted Jan. 18, '64. Was wounded severely in left shoulder, at Deep Bottom, Va., Aug. 14, '64. Promoted Sergeant, Sept. 16, '64 ; 1st Sergeant, Jan. 1, '65, and 2d Lieutenant, Co. H, April 25, '65.

When the regiment was ordered to the N. E. District of Va., he was assigned to duty as Provost-Marshal and Assistant Superintendent of Freedmen, for Middlesex County, Va., with Headquarters at Urbanna, which position he held until ordered to be mustered out.

1st Sergeant George Day entered service as Private, was promoted Corporal October 1, '64 ; Sergeant, January 1, '65 ; 1st Sergeant, May 7, '65.

1st Sergeant Timothy McGraw entered service as Private, reenlisted January 27, '64; was wounded at Deep Run, Va., August 16, '64; was promoted Corporal December 1, '64 ; Sergeant, February 1, '65, and 1st Sergeant, June 12, '65.

Sergeant Ephraim Francis entered service as Corporal; was promoted Sergeant March 28, '62. During the greater part of his term of service he was a victim of ill health, but his faithful care of the sick and his careful attention to the wants of the camp while the Company was on active duty at the front, endeared him to all his comrades.

Sergeant Gardiner E. Blake entered service as Private, was promoted Sergeant September 10, '62. While the regiment was at Fernandina, Fla., from June 5, '63, to Oct. 6, '63, he was Sergeant of the Provost-Guard.

He was taken prisoner at Bermuda Hundred, Va., June 2, '64; was taken to Petersburgh, before the Provost-Marshal, where he was robbed of all his valuables; the following day he was sent to Charleston, S. C., and was put in the city jail, under fire of the Union guns on Morris Island, thence, via Savannah and Macon, to Andersonville Prison, where he was confined until the latter part of August. (We regret that we have no space for the description of the dead line, the scanty rations, the exposure and consequent suffering, disease and death at this prison). From Andersonville he went to the Race Course, two miles north of Charleston, S. C., where he remained three weeks, thence to Florence, S. C. Early in December he was paroled and sent to Annapolis, Md., via Savannah, Ga., where he received a thirty days furlough, from which he reported to Augusta, where he was discharged.

Lieutenant Robert Brady, Jr., entered service as Private; was on detached service at Brigade Headquarters from August 20, '62, to March, '63; was promoted Sergeant January 1, '63; reenlisted January 18, '64; was wounded in left shoulder at Bermuda Hundred, Va., June 2, '64. Though wounded early in the thickest of the fight, he remained with the Company, assisting the new commanding officer to rally the men on the new line, and only when quiet had been restored, did he consent to go to the rear to have his wound dressed. He was also wounded in left arm at Johnson's Plantation, on Darbytown Road, October 29, '64. As Sergeant, he was frequently called upon during the Summer of '64 for perilous service, scouting in front of our lines to obtain information, which service he performed to the entire satisfaction of the Regimental Commander. He was promoted 1st Lieutenant of Company I December 18, '64. Lieutenant Brady commanded Company A from February 10, '65, to March 12, '65. While Captain Rolfe was on furlough, he commanded Company B during the Spring campaign of '65, and Company I from July 1, '65, until mustered out.

When the regiment was ordered to the N. E. District, of Va., he was assigned to duty as Provost-Marshal on the Staff of General Harris, later General Hill, and was especially charged with keeping the peace of the City of Fredericksburgh, which duty he performed in an efficient manner.

Sergeant Alphonzo C. Gowell entered service as Private; reenlisted January 4, '64, was promoted Corporal September 16, '64; Sergeant, January 1, '65; was taken prisoner at Hatcher's Run, Va., April 1, '65.

Sergeant Lyman M. Bragdon entered service as Private; was wounded at Morris Island, S. C., December 8, '63, by the explosion of a rebel shell which broke through the bombproof at the entrance to the Magazine of Battery Chatfield. He was promoted Corporal January 1, '65, and Sergeant, April 18, '65.

Sergeant Jeremiah Stratton entered service as Private. When the regiment left Gloucester Point, Va., for the Spring campaign of '64, he was detailed to guard and store surplus baggage, and while on the passage from Gloucester Point to Norfolk, near Fortress Monroe, May 6, '64, the transport collided with another steamer and sunk. Falling machinery attached to smoke-stack fell across his back and right hip, he was conveyed to hospital at Fortress Monroe, where he remained until about September 1, when he rejoined his Company and regiment, then in front of Petersburgh, Va. Promoted Corporal February 5, '65; wounded at Hatcher's Run, Va., April 2, '65. Promoted Sergeant April 18, '65.

Sergeant Daniel W. Woodbury entered service as Private, was wounded at Darbytown Road, Va., October 13, '64, was promoted Corporal April 18, '65, and Sergeant June 12, '65.

Sergeant Frank E. Young entered service as Private, was promoted Corporal October 13, '65, Sergeant January 1, '66.

Corporal Richard W. Dawe was discharged for disability May 16, '62, at Washington, D. C. Reenlisted December 6, '63, in same Company; was wounded at Bermuda Hundred, Va., June 2, '64, and was discharged by reason of wounds.

Corporal Hughey G. Rideout, after leaving Company D reenlisted Private in Company A, 2d Maine Cavalry, November 30, '63, and died of disease August 11, '64, while in service.

Corporal Freeman R. Dakin was taken prisoner at Fair Oaks, Va., May 31, '62. Was a prisoner with Sergeants Brady, Bassett and others, until November, when he returned to the regiment at Yorktown, where he was discharged. After leaving the Eleventh he again entered service in Company F, 9th Maine Infantry; was wounded in left arm at Bermuda Hundred, Va., and in right elbow at Cold Harbor, Va.

Corporal John Gihn entered service as Private; was promoted Corporal May 16, '62.

Corporal Leonard M. Witham entered service as Private; was promoted Corporal May 16, '62.

Corporal Wm. B. Davis entered service as Private; was promoted Corporal May 16, '62; was discharged for disability at New York, September 23, '62. Reenlisted in 1st D. C. Cavalry; was promoted Sergeant; was taken prisoner September 1, '64; was transferred to Company I, 1st Maine Cavalry, and mustered out July 31, '65.

Died at Insane Hospital, Augusta, Maine, April 20, '87.

Corporal James E. Bailey entered service as Private; was promoted Corporal September 15, '62; reenlisted January 4, '64; was wounded at Bermuda Hundred, Va., June 2, '64. Left arm amputated.

Corporal Patrick Doherty entered service as Private; was promoted Corporal September 15, '62. After leaving the Eleventh he reenlisted as Private in Company H, 30th Maine Infantry, January 6, '64; was taken prisoner at Pleasant Hill, La., April 9, '64; was exchanged and died in service at Bolivar Heights, September 16, '64, just 3 years after his first enlistment in the Eleventh.

Corporal John Dyer entered service as Private; was promoted Corporal October 3, '62. Was accidentally killed in a Shingle Mill, at Springfield, Me., May 23, '69.

Corporal Horace Whittier entered service as Private; was promoted Corporal October 31, '62, and served on Color Guard; was wounded in right breast, at New Market Road, Va., October 7, '64. Was discharged from hospital at Point-of-Rocks, Va.

Corporal Shepard Whittier entered service as Private; was promoted Corporal October 31, '62, and served on Color Guard until October 16, '64, when he was detached for service at Portland, Me., where he was mustered out.

Corporal Stephen R. Bearce entered service as Private, was promoted Corporal October 31, '62; was wounded by the explosion of a rebel shell which broke through the bombproof at the entrance to the Magazine of Battery Chatfield, Morris Island, S. C., December 8, '63; also wounded at Bermuda Hundred, Va., June 17, '64.

1st Sergeant Amaziah Hunter entered service as Private, was promoted Corporal March 27, '63; was commended in orders for volunteering for perilous service in front of the skirmish line, October 7, '64; was mustered out November 18, '64, at expiration of term of service. Reenlisted 1st Sergeant of Company I, December 16, '64; was taken prisoner at Appomattox, Va., April 9, '65, and mustered out June 30, '65.

Corporal Wm. P. Weymouth entered service as Private; was promoted Corporal May 30, '64; was slightly wounded at Deep Bottom, Va., August 14, '64, and after having his wound dressed refused to go to the rear, and returned to the front, where he was again wounded, from the effect of which he died at Fortress Monroe, Va., September 2, '64.

Corporal James B. Williams entered service as Private; was promoted Corporal December 1, '64. Was drowned by the sinking of a boat at South-West Harbor, Me., June 20, '81.

Corporal Jotham S. Annis entered service as Private; reenlisted January 4, '64; was wounded at Drury's Bluff, Va., May 14, '64; promoted Corporal October 13, '65.

Musician Robert A. Strickland was taken prisoner at Fair Oaks, Va., May 31, '62; was a prisoner with Sergeants Brady, Bassett and others until November, '62. He was discharged for disability at Augusta, Me.

Wagoner Henry W. Rider, after being discharged from the Eleventh Maine, reenlisted in Company B, 1st Regiment, Maine Heavy Artillery, December 9, '63; was wounded at Spotsylvania, Va., May 19, '64. Died of wounds May 22, '64.

Bolton, Sumner M., was wounded in right eye and taken prisoner at Bermuda Hundred, Va., June 2, '64. He was taken to Petersburgh, to Popperlane Lawn Hospital, but received no medical treatment, and lost his right eye; thence to Libby Prison. He was exchanged August 13, '64.

Bragdon, Samuel A., was wounded at Bermuda Hundred, Va., June 2, '64, and at Deep Bottom, Va., August 14, '64.

Bryant, Martin V., was taken prisoner at Bermuda Hundred, Va., June 2, '64; was confined at Andersonville, Ga. and various other places, in company with Sergeant Blake, until December, '64, when he was paroled and sent North.

Butler, Alfred C., was wounded in three places at Deep Bottom, Va., August 14, '64; right leg amputated, one arm totally disabled, the other badly wounded.

Butler, George L., was severely wounded at Bermuda Hundred, Va., in the night attack, May 17, '64. Died of wounds at Fortress Monroe, Va., May 20, '64.

Cain, Henry H., was transferred to Veteran Reserve Corps, April 1, '65.

Collins, Josiah, after leaving the Eleventh reenlisted in Company I, 16th Maine Infantry; was transferred to Company I, 20th Maine Infantry. Mustered out July 16, '65.

Cross, Simon, after leaving the Eleventh reenlisted in Company H, 1st Maine Cavalry, December 31, '63. Died in service at Bealton Station, Va., Feb. 5, '64.

Davis, Thomas A., was detached on Western gunboat service, February 17, '62, and served in the Mississippi squadron, was discharged '63. Reenlisted as Corporal in Company L, 2d Maine Cavalry. December 12, '63, and was killed in action at Marianna, Fla., September 27, '64.

Gibbs, Elisha W., died at Eureka, Cal.

Gray, Daniel, was not seen after the Battle of Fair Oaks, Va., May 31, '62. It is probable that when the Company fell back from the advanced position they at first occupied, he joined some other command, as did many others of the Company, and was killed and buried without being recognized. One of the unknown dead.

Haegen, Ira B., was transferred to Vet. Res. Corps. April 1, '64.

House, Mathew P., was taken prisoner at Fair Oaks, Va., May 31, '62 ; was a prisoner with Sergeants Brady, Bassett and others until November, '62, when he returned to the regiment. He was mustered out at expiration of term of service.

Hutchinson, Eleazer, after leaving the Eleventh Maine reenlisted in Company K, 17th Maine Infantry, August 28, '63 ; was wounded May 6, '64 ; was transferred to Company K, 1st Maine Heavy Artillery, and discharged for disability, June 16, '65.

Kelley, Lawrence, was taken prisoner at Bermuda Hundred, Va., June 2, '64. Died in Prison at Andersonville, Ga.

Laffin, Pierce, was wounded at Morris Island, S. C., December 25, '63, by a rebel shell striking a musket and throwing it against his left leg, the bayonet entering the leg some six inches below the knee and taking an upward course shattered the knee.

Lane, Otis, Company cook, while carrying rations to the men employed in felling trees at Bermuda Hundred, Va., May 24, '64, was struck by a falling tree which broke his leg. He died at Biddeford, Me.

Maddox, Greenlief, was wounded at Morris Island, S. C., December 8, '63, by the explosion of a rebel shell which broke through the bombproof at the entrance to the magazine of Battery Chatfield.

Morrill, Charles F., after leaving service settled in Pittsfield, Me. He was killed by being caught in a balance wheel while sawing wood with a horse power at Detroit, Me., April 6, '82.

Philbrook, David C., after leaving the Eleventh reenlisted August 13, '63, private in Company A, 3d Me. Infantry. He was wounded and taken prisoner at Spotsylvania, Va., May 5, '64. At the muster out of the 3d Me., June 4, '64, he was transferred to Company F, 17th Me. and at the muster out of the 17th, June 4, '65, was transferred to the 1st Me. H. A. His death in prison at Andersonville, Ga., August, 64, is asserted by a fellow prisoner, Mr. Oscar Thomas, of Lee, Me.

Sherman, Moses E., was taken prisoner at Fair Oaks, Va., May 31, '62 ; was a prisoner with Sergeants Brady, Bassett and others until November, '62, when he returned to the regiment. Reenlisted January 4, '64; wounded at Bermuda Hundred, Va., June 2, '64. Killed at Appomattox, Va., April 9, '65.

Sherman, William, was taken prisoner at Fair Oaks, Va., May 31, '62 ; was a prisoner with Sergeants Brady, Bassett and others until November, '62, when he returned to the regiment. Reenlisted January 4, '64; wounded at Deep Bottom, Va., August 14, '64, and died of wounds at Fortress Monroe, Va., September 1, '64.

Woodman, Hiram A., was transferred to Vet. Res. Corps, September 1, '63, retransferred to Company D, 11th Me. early in 1864, and served until expiration of his term of service. Was commended in orders for volunteering for perilous service in front of the skirmish line October 7, '64, after the term of his enlistment had expired.

The record of those on roll of D at Muster-out of regiment was :

Killed, - - - - -	'8
Died of Wounds, - - - -	8
Died of Disease, - - - -	32
Discharged Wounded, - - - -	10
Discharged for other Disability, - -	55
Discharged by order, - - - -	2
Transferred, - - - -	1
Resigned, - - - - -	5
Deserted, - - - - -	4
Mustered Out, - - - -	63
In Service, - - - -	26
	214

Of the 214 on the roll of D, we have the

P. O. Address of - - - -	110
Died in Service, - - - -	48
Died since leaving the Eleventh, - -	33
Deserted, - - - -. -	4
Unaccounted for, - - - -	19
	214

Information received after printing Roster.

ADDRESSES :

Corporal John Sherman,	- - -	Rockville, Canada.
Corporal John Gihn,	- - -	Tawas City, Mich.
Corporal James E. Dow, *alias* C. L. Farnsworth,	-	Jonesport, Me.

DEATHS :

Corporal Alphonzo O. Donnell, Died Nov. 21, '83, at Big Rapids, Mich.
Private Thomas R. Blaine, - - - - Died.

Error in Roster.

Curtis, John F., printed John T.

www.ingramcontent.com/pod-product-compliance
Lightning Source LLC
Chambersburg PA
CBHW020326090426
42735CB00009B/1422